DISCOVERING CAREERS FOR YOUR FUTURE

adventure

SECOND EDITION

Ferguson
An imprint of Infobase Publishing

Ferguson
An imprint of Infobase Publishing
132 West 31st Street
New York NY 10001

Library of Congress Cataloging-in-Publication Data

Discovering careers for your future. Adventure. — 2nd ed.
    p. cm.
  Includes bibliographical references and index.
  ISBN-13: 978-0-8160-7290-3 (alk. paper)
  ISBN-10: 0-8160-7290-6 (alk. paper)
  1. Vocational guidance—Juvenile literature. 2. Adventure and adventurers—Vocational guidance—Juvenile literature. [1. Adventure and adventurers—Vocational guidance. 2. Vocational guidance.] I. Ferguson Publishing. II. Title: Adventure.
  HF5381.2.D57 2008
  331.702—dc22
                                  2007045489

Ferguson books are available at special discounts when purchased in bulk quantities for businesses, associations, institutions, or sales promotions. Please call our Special Sales Department in New York at (212) 967-8800 or (800) 322-8755.

You can find Ferguson on the World Wide Web at http://www.fergpubco.com

Text design by Mary Susan Ryan-Flynn
Cover design by Jooyoung An

Printed in the United States of America

EB MSRF 10 9 8 7 6 5 4 3 2 1

This book is printed on acid-free paper.

Contents

Introduction

You may not have decided yet what you want to be in the future. And you don't have to decide right away. You do know that right now you are interested in adventure. Do any of the statements below describe you? If so, you may want to begin thinking about what a career in some type of adventure might mean for you.

___Physical education is my favorite subject in school.
___I like to solve puzzles.
___I like riddles and brain teasers.
___I like all kinds of physical activity.
___I like movies about danger and risk.
___I like to read detective stories and spy stories.
___I enjoy amusement park rides.
___I am interested in extreme sports, such as skysurfing, snowboarding, and bungee jumping.
___I spend a lot of time outdoors.
___I like to explore new places.
___I would like to travel to other countries.
___I am curious and ask a lot of questions.
___I am good at handling stressful situations.
___I can think on my feet and react quickly.
___I am not easily frightened.
___I am good at reading maps and navigating.
___I enjoy activities like scavenger hunts and road rallies.

Discovering Careers for Your Future: Adventure is a book about careers in adventure, from adventure travel specialists to stunt performers. People who have careers in adventure take risks.

Their work usually requires a lot of physical activity. Adventure careers are about exploration, investigation, and discovery, and often involve some physical danger. If you choose a career in adventure, you not only have to be physically strong, but mentally tough, too.

This book describes many possibilities for future careers in adventure. Read through it and see how the different careers are connected. For example, if you are interested in exploration, you will want to read the chapters on adventure travel specialists, astronauts, divers, and tour guides. If you are interested in investigation, you will want to read the chapters on foreign correspondents, private investigators, secret service special agents, and spies. If danger intrigues you, read the chapters on air marshals, bounty hunters, firefighters, and stunt performers. Go ahead and explore!

What Do They Do?

The first section of each chapter begins with a heading such as "What Astronauts Do" or "What Anthropologists Do." It tells what it's like to work at this job. It describes typical responsibilities and assignments. You will find out about working conditions. Which careers involve desk work? Which ones involve working outdoors in all kinds of weather? What tools and equipment are used? This section answers all these questions.

How Do I Prepare for a Career in Adventure?

The section called "Education and Training" tells you what schooling you need for employment in each job—a high school diploma, training at a junior college, a college degree, or more. It also talks about on-the-job training that you could expect to receive after you're hired, and whether or not you must complete an apprenticeship program.

How Much Do People in Adventure Careers Earn?

The Earnings section gives the average salary figures for the job described in the chapter. These figures provide you with a general idea of how much money people with this job can make. Keep in mind that many people really earn more or less than the amounts given here because actual salaries depend on many different things, such as the size of the company, the location of the company, and the amount of education, training, and experience you have. Generally, but not always, bigger companies located in major cities pay more than smaller ones in smaller cities and towns, and people with more education, training, and experience earn more. Also remember that these figures are current averages. They will probably be different by the time you are ready to enter the workforce.

What Will the Future Be Like for Careers in Adventure?

The Outlook section discusses the employment outlook for each career: whether the total number of people employed in this career will increase or decrease in the coming years and whether jobs in this field will be easy or hard to find. These predictions are based on economic conditions, the size and makeup of the population, foreign competition, and new technology. Phrases such as "faster than the average," "about as fast as the average," and "slower than the average" are used by the U.S. Department of Labor to describe job growth predicted by government data.

Keep in mind that these predictions are general statements. No one knows for sure what the future will be like. Also remember that the employment outlook is a general statement about an industry and does not necessarily apply to everyone. A determined and talented person may be able to find a job in an industry or career with the worst kind of outlook. And a person without ambition and the proper training will find it difficult to find a job in even a booming industry or career field.

Where Can I Find More Information?

Each chapter includes a sidebar called "For More Info." It lists organizations that you can contact to find out more about the field and careers in the field. You will find names, addresses, phone numbers, e-mail addresses, and Web sites.

Extras

Every chapter has a few extras. There are photos that show workers in action. There are sidebars and notes on ways to explore the field, fun facts, profiles of people in the field, or lists of resources that might be helpful. At the end of the book you will find three additional sections: Glossary, Index of Job Titles, and Browse and Learn More. The Glossary gives brief definitions of words that relate to education, career training, or employment that you may be unfamiliar with. The Index of Job Titles includes all the job titles mentioned in the book. The Browse and Learn More section lists adventure books and Web sites to explore.

It's not too soon to think about your future. We hope you discover several possible career choices. Happy hunting!

Adventure Travel Specialists

What Adventure Travel Specialists Do

Adventure travel specialists plan, and sometimes lead, tours of unusual, exotic, remote, or wilderness places. Most adventure travel involves some physical activity that takes place outdoors. There are two kinds of adventure travel—*hard* and *soft adventure*. Hard adventure involves high physical activity and advanced skill. Some examples of hard adventure are mountain biking, white-water rafting, or rock climbing. Soft adventure, such as hot air ballooning, horseback riding, or bird watching, is less physical and more family oriented.

A popular type of adventure travel is the ecotour. This kind of trip combines the exciting thrill of adventure with travel to natural areas that conserve the environment and respect the well-being of the local people. Tours of the Asian rainforests, treks to the Amazon jungle, or trips to the Galapagos Islands are some examples of ecotours.

Some adventure travel specialists work in offices planning trips. They make transportation arrangements, order supplies, arrange lodging, and oversee all other details for a successful vacation. They also promote and sell tour packages. Specialists who lead

Americans Love Adventure

One-half of U.S. adults, or 98 million people, have taken an adventure trip in the past five years. Thirty-one million adults participated in hard adventure activities like white-water rafting, scuba diving, and mountain biking.

Source: *Adventure Travel Report*

5

EXPLORING

○ Read magazines, such as *Outside, Backpacker, National Geographic Adventure,* and *Bicycling.*

○ Research environmental groups, such as the National Audubon Society (http://www.audubon.org), National Wildlife Federation (http://www.nwf.org), and Sierra Club (http://www.sierraclub.org).

○ Explore hobbies, such as scuba diving, sailing, hiking, mountain biking, canoeing, or fishing. Check your local phone directory for clubs and organizations that focus on these specialties.

○ Another way to explore this field is to go on an adventure outing yourself. Outward Bound USA (http://www.outwardbound.com), for example, offers a wide variety of programs for teenagers, college students, and adults.

the tours are called *outfitters.* Some adventure specialists both plan and lead tours.

Outfitters and guides demonstrate any activities involved on the trip, help with the equipment, or assist any group member having difficulties. They also speak about the location, scenery, history, wildlife, and unusual aspects of the region where the group is traveling. Guides help tour members in emergency situations or during unplanned events. They are prepared to handle injuries, dangerous areas, and crisis situations.

Education and Training

High school classes such as geography, social studies, and history will prepare you for work as an adventure travel specialist. Speech or English classes will improve your public speaking skills. If you specialize in ecotravel, then study subjects such as earth science, biology, geology, and anthropology. A college degree is not required, but many companies prefer to hire those who have earned one, especially a degree in health, physical education, or recreation. If you plan to manage your own travel business someday, you should take a class in business administration, either at a university or a trade school.

Your experience and skill in a physical activity is important in this career. Take classes or join clubs in your area of interest,

What Is an Ecotourist?

An ecotourist's idea of a perfect vacation is not sitting by the pool sipping lemonade. According to the International Ecotourism Society, ecotourists look for "responsible travel to natural areas that conserves the environment and sustains the well-being of local people." Here's a profile of the average ecotourist:

○ average age is between 35 and 54 years old

○ even percentages of men and women enjoy ecotravel

○ 82 percent are college graduates

○ 60 percent prefer to travel as a couple, 15 percent with families, and 13 percent alone

○ ecotourists prefer long trips—8 to 14 days

○ they don't pinch pennies—26 percent are willing to spend $1,000 to $1,500 per trip

○ the top three tours of choice are: wilderness setting, wildlife viewing, and hiking or trekking

such as rock climbing, ballooning, or photographing wildlife. Certain activities, such as scuba diving, may require formal training and a license examination. All travel guides should have training in emergency first aid and CPR.

Earnings

According to one university offering programs in adventure travel, graduates can make between $125 and $225 per day, or $17,000 for a three- to four-month season. Experienced guides with some managerial responsibilities can earn up to $65,000 a year. Tour leaders receive free food and accommodations, as well as a daily allowance while conducting a tour.

FOR MORE INFO

For industry information, contact
Adventure Travel Trade Association
601 Union Street, 42nd Floor
Seattle, WA 98101-2327
Tel: 360-805-3131
http://www.adventuretravel.biz

For information on the ecotourism industry and related careers, contact
The International Ecotourism Society
1333 H Street NW Suite 300,
East Tower
Washington, D.C. 20005
Tel: 202-347-9203
E-mail: info@ecotourism.org
http://www.ecotourism.org

Visit the OIA's Web site for the latest press releases and adventure travel news.
Outdoor Industry Association (OIA)
4909 Pearl East Circle, Suite 200
Boulder, CO 80301-2499
Tel: 303-444-3353
E-mail: info@outdoorindustry.org
http://www.outdoorindustry.org

Outlook

There is a growing demand for adventure travel. This is because more people are interested in the environment and conservation, as well as physical fitness. There is a lot of competition for adventure travel jobs. Hundreds of people may apply for a single job. Those with experience in adventure travel or a unique specialty will have the best chances for employment.

Air Marshals

What Air Marshals Do

Air marshals, also called *security agents,* have the demanding job of protecting airline passengers and staff from on-board terrorist threats, such as hijackings or bombs. These workers are often covert in their operations, meaning they may be dressed and seated like an average passenger.

Much information about air marshals is classified to protect national security, including details such as their exact number and identities, routes, and training procedures. However, this job is much like that of a Secret Service Special Agent. They must be attentive to all activity that goes on around them, identify potential threats to security, and deal with dangerous individuals or objects on board.

The job of air marshals can be extremely stressful. These workers must be prepared to overcome an attacker (who may be ready to die for his or her cause), all in a confined space without risking harm to any of the plane's passengers. In addition, air marshals must spend considerable time away from home.

Did You Know?

○ The average air marshal flies 181 days per year.

○ Air marshals fly about 15 days per month.

○ Most air marshals spend approximately 900 hours in an aircraft per year.

○ Air marshals spend five hours in an aircraft each day they are on duty.

Source: Transportation Security Administration

EXPLORING

○ Since air marshals work under-cover, you won't be able to observe them at work. You can learn about other airport security workers by watching these people at work your next time at the airport. Although you should not talk to these screeners and other security staff while they are working, you may be able to schedule an interview with security personnel when they are on break or perhaps over the phone.

○ You can also learn about security jobs at your local library or online. Explore the Web site of the Federal Aviation Administration (http://www.faa.gov) for facts and job descriptions, changes in policy, and even summer camp opportunities.

Education and Training

To work as an air marshal, you should have at least a high school diploma. While in high school, take classes in history and government to familiarize yourself with previous events and political threats that have endangered our national security, such as hijackers and terrorist operations. Math classes can be beneficial because, as a security worker, you must be analytical and observant in order to identify and eliminate dangers before problems arise.

Air marshals are highly trained before starting their jobs. They receive rigorous training in classified training centers across the country, and come to the job with previous on-the-job experience in a military or civilian police force. Some of the topics in which they receive training include criminal terrorist behavior recognition, investigative techniques, firearms proficiency, aircraft-specific tactics, and self-defense measures in close quarters.

Earnings

Salaries for air marshals range from approximately $35,000 for new workers to $80,000 or more for the most experienced workers.

Outlook

With the new awareness of airline dangers following the September 11, 2001 terrorist attacks, the public will continue to

To Be a Successful Air Marshal, You Should . . .

○ be calm when under pressure

○ be able to act quickly and intelligently during dangerous situations

○ have good vision and hearing

○ be in good physical shape to face and dominate potential attackers

rely on air marshals for protection from terrorists and other dangers. There will always be a critical need for qualified and skilled individuals to protect airplanes and passengers from security threats.

FOR MORE INFO

The FAA offers a wealth of information on its Web site. Visit the Education & Research pages for information on summer camps for middle and high school students interested in aviation careers.
Federal Aviation Administration (FAA)
800 Independence Avenue SW
Washington, D.C. 20591
Tel: 866-835-5322
http://www.faa.gov

According to its Web site, the TSA "sets the standard for excellence in transportation security through its people, processes, and technologies."
Transportation Security Administration (TSA)
http://www.tsa.gov

Anthropologists

What Anthropologists Do

Anthropologists study humans and how they have developed over hundreds of thousands of years. They are interested in the lifestyles and customs of groups of people in all parts of the world.

Cultural anthropologists study human behavior and culture. They look for things that will tell them about a people's religion, language, politics, or art. They interview people and observe them in their daily lives to learn about their customs, habits, and beliefs. Some anthropologists learn about the culture of a particular group of people by studying their weapons, tools, and pottery. Others study their language.

Physical anthropologists study the physical differences between people of past and present human societies. They compare human skeletal remains and the environments where they were

Profile: Margaret Mead

Margaret Mead (1901–1978) was a pioneer in cultural anthropology. She performed many studies of child-training methods. She studied the development of adolescents in the Samoan and Admiralty islands, which she described in the books *Coming of Age in Samoa* (1928) and *Growing Up in New Guinea* (1930). Later in her career she wrote about child development, personality formation, family life, feminism, cultural change, and national character (the customary attitudes of a people).

Margaret Mead received a Ph.D. degree from Columbia University in 1929. She joined the ethnology staff of the American Museum of Natural History in New York City in 1928 and was curator of ethnology from 1964 to 1969. While on the museum's staff, she made a number of expeditions to the South Pacific islands and taught at Columbia and Fordham universities.

An anthropologist interviews villagers in Bundu Tuhan, Malaysia. (Michael Doolittle, The Image Works)

found to trace the origin of different peoples. Many physical anthropologists also study other primates, such as chimpanzees and gorillas.

Urban anthropologists study the behavior and customs of people who live in cities. *Ethnologists* study tribal cultures that live in remote regions of the world.

Most anthropologists work for colleges, universities, or museums. They spend part of their time teaching anthropology, geography, or sociology. They may set up exhibits or catalog and store artifacts.

Some anthropologists travel a lot and are away from home for long periods of time. They sometimes live in remote areas of the world or in unfamiliar conditions. Anthropologists spend long hours taking notes, doing research, and writing about their work.

Education and Training

If you are interested in anthropology, concentrate on classes in history, English, writing, religion, foreign language, and art in high school.

EXPLORING

- ○ Participate in boys' or girls' clubs that offer exploration and camping trips.
- ○ Learn about other cultures by attending local cultural festivals, music and dance performances, and religious ceremonies.
- ○ Visit cultural centers and museums of natural history.
- ○ Start thinking about the Earthwatch Institute's opportunities for high school students. Its Student Challenge Awards program offers selected students a chance to assist in the summer research of scientists. Recent projects included an archaeological study with computer imaging at an ancestral Hopi village in northern Arizona. Check out the Earthwatch Institute's Web site for more information (http://www.earthwatch.org).

Some beginning jobs in anthropology may be open to those who have bachelor's or master's degrees, but most anthropologists go on to earn a doctoral degree. There are many graduate schools that offer strong programs in anthropology and archaeology.

Earnings

According to the U.S. Department of Labor, college and university anthropology professors earned between $37,590 and $109,330 in 2006, depending on the type of institution.

For those who do not work at colleges and universities, the salaries vary widely. The U.S. Department of Labor reports that the median annual salary for anthropologists was $49,930 in 2006. Salaries ranged from less than $28,940 to $81,490 or more.

Outlook

Most new jobs in the anthropology field in the near future will be non-teaching positions in management, scientific, and technical consulting services.

College and university teaching has been the largest area of employment for anthropologists in the past. The demand for professors is expected to decline. Competition for teaching positions will be great even for those with doctorates.

To Be a Successful Anthropologist, You Should . . .

○ be able to work as part of a team and do research on your own

○ be very curious and like to learn new things

○ be very dedicated to your work

○ respect other cultures

○ have excellent communication skills

Employment for anthropologists in both teaching and nonteaching positions should grow about as fast as average, according to the U.S. Department of Labor.

FOR MORE INFO

The following organization offers valuable information about anthropological careers and student associations.

American Anthropological Association
2200 Wilson Boulevard, Suite 600
Arlington, VA 22201-3357
Tel: 703-528-1902
www.aaanet.org

The SfAA's Web site has career listings and publications for those wanting to read more about current topics in the social sciences.

Society for Applied Anthropology (SfAA)
PO Box 2436
Oklahoma City, OK 73101-2436
Tel: 405-843-5113
E-mail: info@sfaa.net
http://www.sfaa.net

Archaeologists

What Archaeologists Do

Archaeologists study the physical evidence of people who lived in ancient times. They excavate, or dig up, the remains of ancient settlements, such as tools, clay pottery, clothing, weapons, and ornaments. They identify and study them to learn more about what life was like in the past.

Archaeologists often travel to places where ancient cultures once flourished. At the site, they carefully dig up any objects (artifacts) or remains of people, plants, and animals (realia) that remain from the culture. They try to clean, repair, and restore the artifacts as nearly as possible to their original condition. They study the realia to figure out what they looked like, what the people ate, how and where they lived, and how they survived.

Archaeologists must keep careful records. It is important to know exactly where each item was found and what its condition was. This can be very tedious work. Usually, when an archaeology team excavates an area, they brush the layer of dirt off one inch at a time with paintbrushes, toothbrushes, and soft bristles. They save all the sand and dirt that they have brushed away. Another member of the team sifts this

Where Archaeologists Work

○ colleges and universities

○ museums

○ historic sites

○ federal and state government agencies such as the U.S. Forest Service, National Park Service, Bureau of Land Management, and the U.S. Army Corps of Engineers

○ state historic preservation offices

○ engineering firms with cultural resource management divisions

○ cultural resource management companies

○ self-employment

Source: Society for American Archaeology

An archaeologist uses a trowel to excavate a historical site in North Dakota.
(Robert Etzel, U.S. Army Corps of Engineers)

dirt with a fine screen to find any tiny bone fragments or chips of pottery.

In addition to research, archaeologists teach in colleges or universities or work in museums. Teachers give lectures, correct papers, and take students on field trips. Museum workers may also give lectures, as well as plan museum exhibits and work with the other members of the museum staff.

Education and Training

It takes years of study and special training to become an archaeologist. In high school, you should study as many modern and dead languages as possible. Classes in English, writing, history, and social studies will be most helpful.

EXPLORING

○ Read books and magazines about archaeology. One useful magazine for kids is *Dig* (http://www.digon site.com).
○ Join scouting troops and other youth organizations that go exploring on camping trips.
○ Visit nearby museums to see archaeological exhibits. Listen to lectures and talk to museum archaeologists to find out more about archaeology as a career.

Interesting Web Sites

About.com: Archaeology
http://archaeology.about.com

Archaeological Parks in the U.S.
http://www.uark.edu/misc/aras

Archaeology
http://www.archaeology.org

Archaeology and You
http://www.saa.org/publications/ArchAndYou

The Archaeology Channel
http://www.archaeologychannel.org

National Park Service: Archeology Program
http://www.nps.gov/archeology

Passport in Time
http://www.passportintime.com

A bachelor's degree is the minimum requirement after high school. Most archaeologists have also earned a doctorate. If you want to be an archaeologist, you should enjoy

Additional Opportunities in Archaeology

- archaeobotanist
- computer specialist in archaeology
- cultural resource lawyer
- editor
- field supervisor
- field technician
- geographic information systems specialist
- laboratory supervisor
- manager, cultural resource firm
- writer

Source: About.com

reading, studying, and writing, and have a strong interest in history.

Earnings

Archaeologists who work as professors earn incomes that ranged from less than $37,590 to $109,330 or more a year in 2006, according to the U.S. Department of Labor. Experienced archaeologists who do not work at colleges and universities earned annual salaries that ranged from less than $28,940 to $81,490 or more a year in 2006.

Outlook

Most archaeologists work for colleges and universities, but in the future, there will be fewer teaching jobs available. This means that more archaeologists will look for work at research companies, government agencies, and large corporations. The fields of environmental protection and historical preservation are growing, providing more jobs for archaeologists. An increasing number of archaeologists will be employed by construction companies to perform salvage archaeology, in which artifacts are excavated quickly before construction destroys a historical site.

FOR MORE INFO

At the AAA's Web site, you can find valuable information about archaeology careers.

American Anthropological Association (AAA)
2200 Wilson Boulevard, Suite 600
Arlington, VA 22201-3357
Tel: 703-528-1902
www.aaanet.org

For information on archaeological careers including answers to frequently asked questions about the field, contact
Society for American Archaeology
900 2nd Street NE, Suite 12
Washington, D.C. 20002-3560
Tel: 202-789-8200
E-mail: headquarters@saa.org
http://www.saa.org

Astronauts

What Astronauts Do

An *astronaut* is a person who is trained to travel in a space-craft. While on missions, astronauts conduct scientific experiments. These experiments help scientists understand how humans can live and work in space. Astronauts may perform experiments on animals, plants, minerals, or themselves to study the effects of weightlessness or other conditions in space. Sometimes they operate laboratories on board the spacecraft to learn more about astronomy or earth sciences. Much of the research done is useful for medical purposes, such as finding cures for diseases.

Astronauts participate in mission training in one of the high fidelity trainers/ mockups at the Johnson Space Center. (National Aeronautics and Space Administration)

At National Aeronautics and Space Administration (NASA) training centers, astronauts go through extensive training to prepare for work in space. The human body works differently in the zero gravity of outer space, so astronauts have to undergo many tests to make sure their bodies can handle the changes. These tests are conducted in simulators, machines designed to mimic what outer space is like.

The crew of a space shuttle is made up of a *commander,* a *pilot,* and three or more other crewmembers. The commander is in control of the mission. The pilot helps the commander fly the shuttle and may help handle satellites. The other crewmembers, called *mission specialists,* work on experiments, launch satellites, and carry out other duties necessary to the mission. One or more *payload specialists* may also be included on flights. A payload specialist may not be a NASA astronaut but is an expert on the cargo being carried into space.

Education and Training

If you are interested in a career as an astronaut, you should follow a regular college-preparatory curriculum in high school and be sure to take as many courses as possible in mathematics and science.

If you want to become an astronaut, plan to attend college. NASA requires astronauts to have a degree in engineering,

EXPLORING

○ NASA's Web site (http://nasajobs. nasa.gov/astronauts) has a special section for students that includes biographies of astronauts, advice on becoming an astronaut, and news about current NASA projects. Another Web site, Ask the Space Scientist (http://image.gsfc. nasa.gov/poetry/ask/askmag.html), allows you to e-mail questions to an astronomer who answers questions online.

○ Visiting the National Air and Space Museum at the Smithsonian Institution in Washington, D.C., is an excellent way to learn about space exploration history. There are also several NASA-run space, research, and flight centers throughout the United States. Most have visitor centers and offer tours.

○ Space camps are conducted all over the country during the summer. They are an excellent way to learn more about astronauts. Ask a counselor or science teacher at your school to help you learn more about space camps if you are interested.

biology, physical science, or mathematics. Astronauts also often have doctorates in the natural sciences, engineering, or medicine. Some astronauts have military backgrounds instead, but still must have knowledge in sciences. Astronauts also must be U.S. citizens and pass the NASA physical, which includes certain height and vision requirements.

Astronauts are trained in all aspects of space flight. They receive classroom instruction in astronomy, physics, star navigation, communications, computers, rocket engines and fuels, and space medicine. They train in space flight simulators, which mimic space flight so that astronauts can practice procedures, train for emergencies, and experience changes in air pressure and temperature.

Earnings

Astronauts earn beginning salaries in accordance with the U.S. government pay scale. Astronauts enter the field at a minimum classification of GS-11, which in 2007 paid at least $46,974, according to the Office of Personnel Management

Beginnings

When the U.S. space program began in 1959, there were only seven astronauts in the entire country. As of 2007, there were 95 astronauts and 11 candidates in the U.S. space program. In total, 321 astronauts have been selected in the 19 groups from 1959 through 2004. The first person to travel in space was a Russian, Yuri A. Gagarin, on April 12, 1961. The United States quickly followed, launching Alan Shepard, the first U.S. astronaut, into space on May 5, 1961. These men may have been the first to experience space, but the work of other pioneers made space travel possible. Robert H. Goddard (1882–1945) of the United States and Hermann Oberth (1894–1989) of Germany are known as the fathers of space flight. Goddard designed and built a number of rocket motors and ground-tested the liquid fuel rocket. Oberth published *The Rocket into Interplanetary Space* in 1923, which discussed technical problems of space and described what a spaceship would be like.

General Schedule. As they gain experience, astronauts may move up the classification chart to peak at GS-13, which pays between $66,951 and $87,039.

Outlook

There is a lot of competition for astronaut jobs. Thousands of men and women apply for openings, but only 100 are chosen for the training program every few years. Future need for new astronauts will depend on the success of the existing program, the International Space Station (ISS), and on new projects (such as the Constellation Program—which will create a new spacecraft, the Crew Exploration Vehicle, by 2011 that will be used to ferry astronauts and cargo to the ISS and explore the Moon, Mars, and beyond).

FOR MORE INFO

For information on space launches, the International Space Station, and other educational resources, contact

Kennedy Space Center
Tel: 321-867-5000
http://www.ksc.nasa.gov

For information on careers, internships, and student projects, contact the information center or visit NASA's Web site.

National Aeronautics and Space Administration (NASA)
Public Communications and Inquiries
Management Office
Washington, D.C. 20546-0001
Tel: 202-358-0001
E-mail: public-inquiries@hq.nasa.gov
http://www.nasa.gov

Bounty Hunters

What Bounty Hunters Do

Bounty hunters, sometimes called *bail enforcement agents* or *fugitive recovery agents,* track down and return people who are fugitives from justice. They work with bail bondsmen and the court system. When people are arrested, they can sometimes get out of jail if they guarantee they will appear in court on a certain date by posting a large amount of money, called bail. If they appear in court as they promised, the bail money is returned. Most people who are arrested don't have large sums of money, so they use the services of a bail bondsman who provides the money to the court. The person pays the bondsman a fee—usually 10 percent of the actual posted bond. If the person does not show up on the court date, the court allows 90 to 180 days for the bondsman to bring the person in or hire a bounty hunter to track down the person. The bounty hunter is paid only if the fugitive is returned to court.

Bounty Hunters on TV

The Lone Ranger began airing in 1949 and portrayed a ranger and his sidekick Tonto cleaning up the Old West.

Bounty Hunter aired in the late 1950s and showed bounty hunting as a respectable career. Steve McQueen starred in the series.

Gunsmoke depicted the bounty hunter as lawless. The main character, Matt Dillon, often fought against the ruthless bounty hunter.

Walker, Texas Ranger showed a modern-day ranger (played by Chuck Norris), an updated version of the original Texas Rangers that tracked down lawbreakers in the Texas territory.

The bounty hunter's main goal is to find the fugitive as quickly and safely as possible. Bounty hunters use research, detection, and law enforcement skills. They interview people, trace papers, such as credit card receipts, and spend hours in surveillance. Bounty hunters can use almost any means possible to re-arrest a fugitive. In most states they can enter the homes of fugitives if they believe beyond a reasonable doubt that the fugitive is inside. Most bounty hunters use weapons both to persuade fugitives to return peacefully and to protect themselves. After the fugitive is found, the bounty hunter arrests the individual and takes the fugitive back to jail to await trial.

Education and Training

In high school, classes in government, political science, communication, and business will help you prepare for the legal and business side of bounty hunting. Self-defense or martial arts courses can give you skills you might need when capturing a fugitive. Foreign languages may come in handy as well, depending on the area of the country where you work.

A college education is not required to become a bounty hunter, but you do need training in law enforcement and criminal justice. A college degree in criminal justice or police academy training is helpful.

EXPLORING

○ Since bounty hunting can be dangerous, it will be difficult to explore this career until you are older and have some experience in law enforcement. You can start now by reading books like these: *Private Investigators and Bounty Hunters* by Ann Gaines (New York: Chelsea House, 1999); and *Bounty Hunters, Marshals, and Sheriffs: Forward to the Past* by Jacqueline Pope (Westport, Conn.: Praeger, 1998). The first book explains the history and cases of private investigators and bounty hunters and discusses how bounty hunters are represented in the media. In the second book, sheriffs, marshals, and bounty hunters are remembered as relics of America's Wild West past.

○ Contact a bail bondsman (you'll find many listed in the phone book) and find out if they are also bounty hunters. Ask any questions you may have. Try to interview several bondsmen to get a more balanced view of what it's like to work in the bail bonding and fugitive recovery business.

It's a Fact

The history of the bail process dates back to English common law beginning around 1066. People who were charged with crimes against the king were allowed to go free if someone else guaranteed that the individual would return. If that didn't happen, the person who guaranteed the return of the individual often had to pay the price instead.

In America, this process continued and those who offered guarantees for the accused people became known as bail bondsmen and bounty hunters. Bounty hunting grew as a profession during the westward expansion of the United States. Fugitives would often run as far west as possible to get away from local law enforcement, so bounty hunters were often found tracking lawbreakers in the Old West.

Groups of men, called Rangers, gathered to clean up areas of the West, such as Arizona and Texas, as they became part of the Union. These men would "range" over large territories, tracking down and apprehending lawbreakers. Later, most bounty-hunting activities were performed by marshals, sheriffs, and detectives.

Earnings

Bounty hunters who start their own businesses should expect to lose money at the beginning, according to the Fugitive Apprehension Select Team in Missouri. The bounty-hunting business, like any other, takes time to grow. The National Center

Famous Bounty Hunters

○ Pat Garrett tracked down Billy the Kid.

○ Bat Masterson assisted Federal Marshal Wyatt Earp in bringing law and order to Tombstone, Arizona, in the 1880s.

○ The Texas Rangers "thinned out" more than 3,000 Texas desperados in the 1870s.

○ The Arizona Rangers cleaned up the lawlessness of Arizona so that it could become the 48th state of the United States.

for Policy Analysis states that beginning bounty hunters earn $20,000 or more per year, while more established bounty hunters and business owners can earn more than $30,000 per year. According to CNNMoney, bounty hunters generally earn between $40,000 and $60,000 per year. Well-established bail enforcement agents with excellent reputations often get the highest-paying cases, such as for a fugitive who has run on a $100,000 bail, and may find their yearly earnings approaching the $100,000 mark.

Outlook

Employment for bounty hunters will increase about as fast as the average. There is healthy competition among bail enforcement agents. They are a small but important part of our legal system.

FOR MORE INFO

For industry information, contact the following organizations:

American Bail Enforcement Association
PO Box 33244
Austin, TX 78764-0244
Tel: 512-719-3595
http://www.pimall.com/nais/n.dm.html

National Association of Bail Enforcement Agents
PO Box 129
Falls Church, VA 22040-0129
Tel: 703-534-4211
http://www.nabea.org

National Enforcement Agency
PO Box 3540
Gaithersburg, MD 20885-3540
Tel: 866-384-4848
http://nationalbailenforcement.com

National Institute of Bail Enforcement
PO Box 667
Spring Grove, IL 60081-0667
Tel: 815-675-0260
http://www.bounty-hunter.net

Divers

What Divers Do

Divers use scuba gear (an oxygen tank and breathing apparatus) to perform underwater work. They inspect, repair, remove, and install underwater equipment and structures. Some work on underwater scientific research projects. Others build and maintain oil wells and other underwater structures.

Most divers work for commercial diving contractors who take on a wide variety of jobs, such as building underwater foundations for bridges; placing offshore oil well piping; and fixing damaged ships, barges, or permanent structures located in the water.

Divers must be skilled at diving, but they also must be able to do many other tasks both underwater and aboard a sailing vessel.

A military diver emerges from underwater after placing high explosives to clear debris that may affect the movement of ships in a harbor. (Topham, The Image Works)

They may repair a hole in a ship while it is in the water. Some divers work on research projects in marine biology or oceanography. They may take underwater photographs. Some work on salvage projects, exploring and retrieving items from ships wrecked at sea. Others help with underwater military projects.

Diving is very strenuous and may be dangerous. They use diving equipment such as air compressors, breathing-gas storage tanks, and communications equipment. The divers stay in contact with workers on the boat to receive instructions and warnings of danger. They often work as part of a team and must always be aware of what is going on around them and how much oxygen is in their tanks.

EXPLORING

○ You can begin diving training before high school. Between the ages of 10 and 14, you can earn a junior open water diver certification, which allows you to dive in the company of a certified adult. When you turn 15, you can upgrade your certification to open water diver.

○ Learn to feel at home in water and underwater. Join the swim team or take swimming lessons. Practice regularly, outdoors if possible. Hobbies such as boating, fishing, and waterskiing allow you to spend time in and on the water.

The Bends

A big concern for deepwater divers is the added pressure of the water's weight. This pressure causes the nitrogen in the air breathed by the diver to dissolve in the bloodstream. Normally, the nitrogen stays in the lungs and is simply exhaled in the breathing process. But when a diver returns too rapidly from deep water (more than 200 feet deep) to the surface, bubbles of nitrogen form in the blood vessels.

This sickness is called the bends (also known as caisson disease or decompression sickness). The nitrogen bubbles build up in the joints, causing pain in the knees, elbows, hips, or shoulders. If not treated right away, the bends can cause paralysis, coma, and even death.

To prevent the bends, divers must return slowly enough to the surface so that the nitrogen in the blood is exhaled from the lungs normally, instead of being trapped in the blood vessels. To treat the bends, the diver is placed in a decompression chamber. It contains air under high pressure that is gradually reduced to normal.

Diving Perks

Work Half a Year for Full-time Pay
There are about three jobs for every qualified graduate of a technical diving program, so divers get paid rather well. In fact, they are paid so well that many divers choose to work only half a year—the official diving season—from June to December.

Travel the World
In the United States, a great many jobs are located in the Gulf of Mexico and on the Louisiana coastline and many divers choose to live near those areas. However, divers are able to travel to many different places to work on exploratory assignments and they meet many different kinds of people.

Take a Vacation
Graduates of diving programs can teach recreational scuba diving classes. They supervise or teach tourist diving at resorts and vacation spots around the world. The diving instructor is responsible for their safety in the water and for handling any emergencies that might arise.

Source: National Association of Commercial Divers

Some divers and diving technicians are *recreation specialists.* They teach scuba diving lessons or coordinate diving programs for resorts or cruise ships.

Education and Training

The best way to prepare for a diving career is to complete a two-year training program. The two-year program teaches diving techniques and the skills you need to work underwater. Programs for recreation specialists also include training in business and communication. Typical basic requirements for enrollment in a diving program are a high school diploma or its equivalent, reading comprehension, completion of three to four years of language and communications subjects, at least one year of algebra, and one year of physics or chemistry with laboratory work. Of course, you must be an excellent swimmer and have the coordination to perform complicated tasks underwater.

Earnings

The average beginning salary for divers is about $26,000 a year for about six to eight months of work, but earnings increase rapidly with experience. Within four years a skilled diver may earn more than $40,000 a year. Divers may work every day on a project for three months and then have three or four weeks off before they get another job assignment. A few highly experienced divers may make more than $75,000.

Outlook

There are many job opportunities for trained divers. Petroleum companies need diving experts to help them search for oil and natural gas. Shipping companies need them to repair vessels, and research projects need them to take underwater photographs and set up scientific equipment.

FOR MORE INFO

For information on commercial diving and educational programs, contact
Association of Commercial Diving Educators
c/o Santa Barbara City College
721 Cliff Drive
Santa Barbara, CA 93109-2312
Tel: 805-965-0581, ext. 2426
http://www.acde.us

For information on diving instruction and certification, contact
National Association of Underwater Instructors
PO Box 89789
Tampa, FL 33689-0413
Tel: 800-553-6284
E-mail: nauihq@nauiww.org
http://www.nauiww.org

Emergency Medical Technicians

What Emergency Medical Technicians Do

Emergency medical technicians, or *EMTs,* drive in ambulances or fly in helicopters or fixed-wing aircraft to the scene of accidents or emergencies to care for ill or injured people. EMTs decide what kind of medical help victims need and treat them quickly. They may set broken bones or try to restart someone's heart. They must be able to stay calm and to calm others in a crisis.

The ambulances, helicopters, and fixed-wing aircraft EMTs use have two-way radios. At the scene of an emergency, EMTs may need to make radio contact with hospitals to ask for a physician's advice about treatment. On the way to the hospital, EMTs radio ahead so the emergency room is ready. They help

Did You Know?

○ More than 16 million patients are transported by ambulance each year.

○ Approximately 192,000 EMTs and paramedics are employed in the United States.

○ About 40 percent of EMTs and paramedics work for private ambulance services. Thirty percent work in local government for fire departments, emergency medical services, and public ambulance services. And 20 percent work in hospitals.

Sources: National Association of Emergency Medical Technicians, U.S. Department of Labor

carry the victims into the hospital, and give the hospital staff as much information as they can about the patient's condition and the nature of the accident.

EMTs must keep their ambulances and aircraft in good order and make sure that they always have the equipment they need. This includes replacing used linens and blankets and replenishing supplies of drugs and oxygen.

EMTs work for hospitals, fire departments, police departments, private ambulance services, or other first aid organizations. In fire departments, most EMTs work 50 hours a week; in hospitals, between 45 and 60 hours a

An emergency medical technician prepares equipment in order to be ready to respond to her next call. (Bob Daemmrich, The Image Works)

Words to Learn

amkus cutter a handheld rescue device, similar to scissors, used to free trapped victims by cutting through metal

amkus rams a handheld rescue device used to free trapped victims by pushing or pulling obstructions, such as the dashboard and seats, away from the victim

amkus spreader a handheld rescue device used to free trapped victims by pulling apart crumpled metal

backboard a long, flat, hard surface used to immobilize the spine in case of neck or spinal injury

defibrillator a machine with electrodes that is used to apply electric currents to heart muscles in order to shock the muscles into operation

endotracheal intubation the insertion of a tube into the trachea, or windpipe, to provide a passage for air, in case of obstruction

intravenous administered by an injection into the vein

EXPLORING

○ High school health courses are a useful introduction to some of the concepts and terminology that EMTs use.

○ Ask your health teacher to help arrange an information interview with an EMT. Ask the following questions: What are your main and secondary job duties? What do you like least and most about your job? How did you train for this field? What advice would you give a young person who is interested in the field?

○ You may be able to take a first aid class or training in cardiopulmonary resuscitation (CPR). Organizations such as the Red Cross or a nearby hospital can provide information on local training courses.

○ When you get to high school, you may be able to volunteer at hospitals or clinics to learn more about medicine and health care.

week; and in private ambulance services, between 45 and 50 hours. Since people need emergency help at all hours, EMTs work nights, weekends, and holidays.

Education and Training

To be an EMT, you must first finish high school. You have to be at least 18 years old and have a driver's license. High school courses in health, physics, chemistry, and mathematics are helpful. A course in driver's education will be useful because EMTs must have excellent driving skills. You need to know the roads and travel conditions in your area so you can drive to the scene of an emergency and to the hospital quickly and safely.

Many hospitals, colleges, and police and fire departments offer the basic EMT training course. The federal government requires all EMTs to pass this basic training course, which teaches you how to deal with common medical emergencies.

Earnings

EMTs who work in the public sector for police and fire departments usually receive a higher wage than those who work for ambulance companies and hospitals. According to the U.S. Department of Labor, median annual earnings of EMTs and paramedics were $27,070 in 2006. Salaries ranged from less than $17,300 for the lowest 10 percent to more than $45,280 for the highest 10 percent.

Emergency Medical Service Designations

first responder held by professionals (often firefighters and police) with approximately 40 hours of training

EMT-Basic held by professionals with approximately 110 hours of training

EMT-Intermediate held by professionals with approximately 200–400 hours of training

paramedic held by professionals with 1,000 or more hours of training

Source: National Association of Emergency Medical Technicians

Outlook

The employment outlook for EMTs should remain very good in larger communities. In smaller communities with fewer financial resources, the outlook may not be as good. Older people use emergency medical services more often than do younger people; the growing numbers in this sector of the population should increase the need for EMTs. Opportunities will be best for EMTs employed by private ambulance services.

FOR MORE INFO

This organization represents companies that provide emergency and nonemergency medical transportation services.
American Ambulance Association
8201 Greensboro Drive, Suite 300
McLean, VA 22102-3814
Tel: 800-523-4447
http://www.the-aaa.org

For information on EMT careers, contact
National Association of Emergency Medical Technicians
PO Box 1400
Clinton, MS 39060-1400

Tel: 800-346-2368
E-mail: info@naemt.org
http://www.naemt.org

For information on testing for EMT certification, contact
National Registry of Emergency Medical Technicians
Rocco V. Morando Building
6610 Busch Boulevard
PO Box 29233
Columbus, OH 43229-1740
Tel: 614-888-4484
http://www.nremt.org

Firefighters

What Firefighters Do

Firefighters protect people's lives and property from the hazards of fire and other emergencies. They put out fires, and rescue people from burning buildings and accident sites. They hold safety inspections to look for fire dangers and unsafe conditions. Most firefighters are also trained to give emergency medical assistance.

When a fire department gets an emergency call, firefighters have already been assigned their duties. Their tasks may be to find and rescue people, raise ladders, connect hoses to water hydrants, or break down doors or windows so that others can enter the area with water hoses. Commanding officers such as fire captains, battalion chiefs, or the fire chief coordinate and supervise these activities.

After a fire has been put out, *fire investigators* try to find out what caused it. If fire investigators find that a fire was set deliberately, they gather the evidence that proves this, and search for clues about who set the fire, arrest the suspected arsonist, and testify in court.

Fire inspectors prevent fires by inspecting buildings for dangers, such as combustible materials and damaged electrical wiring. They also make sure that buildings comply with fire codes and city ordinances.

Firefighters often work long shifts, spending many hours at a time in the

It's a Fact

○ Today, there are more than 30,000 organized fire departments across the United States, with about 282,000 professional, salaried firefighters.

○ Fire departments responded to an estimated 1,642,500 fires in 2006. These fires resulted in 89 firefighter deaths, 3,245 civilian fire fatalities, 16,400 civilian fire injuries, and more than \$11.3 billion in property loss.

Source: National Fire Protection Association

Profile: Chief Bobby Williams

Chief Bobby Williams works for the Spokane Fire Department in Spokane, Washington. He tells how he became a firefighter and gives some advice on how to become one yourself.

"I grew up in a small town in Chesterfield County, Virginia. My father owned a neighborhood grocery store across the street from the volunteer fire station. He became a volunteer soon after opening the store. In our early teens, my brother and I would go with our father on calls when he drove his own car to fire scenes.

"At 15, I became a junior firefighter. I fell in love with the fire service and knew right away that it was what I wanted to do professionally. I set my goal to become a fire chief of a good-sized community before I was 30 years old.

"To meet that goal, I attended Rowan Technical Institute in Salisbury, North Carolina. I earned my associate of applied science (A.A.S.) degree in fire and safety engineering. During my studies there, I was a resident firefighter. When I graduated, I worked as a paid firefighter for the Chesterfield Fire Department for one year. Then I went on to earn a bachelor's degree in fire protection and a master's degree in business administration from Oklahoma State University.

"Students who are interested in this career need to understand the actual jobs that we perform in the fire service. Many folks are not aware that, for example, about 75 percent of our incidents are of an emergency medical nature. Talk to those who are doing the jobs to get a better idea of what is really involved.

"Next, make sure to find the best formal education programs that offer a major in fire protection. My high school guidance counselor and the local fire chief both encouraged me to go beyond the A.A.S. degree. They knew that employment as a fire chief would require those advanced degrees, and they were right."

station. They must be prepared to answer an alarm call at any moment. In many smaller towns, they may be employed on a part-time basis or serve as volunteers. This means that they are on alarm call from their homes, and sometimes they have to leave during a family meal or in the middle of the night.

Education and Training

In most towns and cities, firefighters are required to be at least 18 years old and have a high school education. Classes in

Women make up a growing percentage of firefighters in the United States. (Michael Okoniewski, The Image Works)

sciences such as anatomy, chemistry, physics, and biology will be helpful.

Some cities require two to four years of college education. Many people who intend to become firefighters attend two-year postsecondary school fire-technology programs, which are offered at junior and community colleges. Applicants usually must pass written tests and meet certain requirements for height, weight, physical fitness, stamina, and vision. Beginning firefighters receive several weeks of intensive training, either on the job or through formal fire department training schools.

Earnings

Beginning salaries for full-time firefighters averaged about $20,660 a

Major Causes of Home Fires, 2000–2004

cooking equipment:	32 percent
heating equipment:	16 percent
arson:	5 percent
candle:	4 percent
smoking materials:	4 percent
exposure to other fire:	4 percent
confined or contained trash or rubbish fire:	4 percent
electrical distribution or lighting equipment:	3 percent
clothing dryer or washer:	2 percent
playing with heat source:	2 percent

Source: National Fire Protection Association

year in 2006, according to the U.S. Department of Labor. Experienced firefighters earned salaries that ranged from $41,190 to $66,140 or more a year. Fire inspectors and investigators earned salaries that ranged from $29,840 to $74,930 or more in 2006. For all positions, earnings vary with the size of the fire department and the location.

Outlook

Employment of firefighters is expected to grow faster than the average, according to the U.S. Department of Labor, as new firefighters are needed to replace those who retire or leave the field. Firefighting is forecasted to remain a very competitive field, and the number of people interested in becoming firefighters will be higher than the number of available positions in most areas.

EXPLORING

○ Take classes in first aid and CPR. Your community may offer these training courses. Also contact the American Red Cross chapter in your area for information on classes.
○ Volunteer for any fire prevention activities offered at your school. Many teachers appoint a student "fire marshal" who is in charge of leading classmates to the proper exits during fire drills and real fire emergencies.
○ Does your family have an evacuation plan for fire emergencies? Talk to your parents about various exit routes and assign specific tasks for each family member, such as calling 911 or helping a grandparent or toddler get out of the house safely.

FOR MORE INFO

For information on careers in the fire service, contact
International Association of Fire Fighters
1750 New York Avenue NW
Washington, D.C. 20006-5301
Tel: 202-737-8484
http://www.iaff.org

For information on fire safety issues, careers in fire protection, and public education, contact
National Fire Protection Association
1 Batterymarch Park
Quincy, MA 02169-7471
Tel: 617-770-3000
http://www.nfpa.org

Foreign Correspondents

What Foreign Correspondents Do

Foreign correspondents report on news from other countries. They work for newspapers, radio or television networks, Internet news services, or wire services. Today's media usually rely on reports from news wire services for international news coverage rather than sending their own reporters to the scene. Only the biggest newspapers and television networks employ foreign correspondents. These reporters are usually stationed in a particular city and cover a wide territory.

Foreign news can range from wars, political takeovers, and refugee situations to cultural events and financial issues. *Domestic correspondents* usually cover one specific area of the news, such as politics, health, sports, consumer affairs, business, or religion. But foreign correspondents usually cover all of these topics in the country where they are stationed. Sometimes a foreign correspondent reports the news from several neighboring countries.

News Pioneers

James Gordon Bennett, Sr. (1795–1872), a U.S. journalist and publisher of the *New York Herald,* was responsible for many firsts in the newspaper industry. He was the first publisher to sell papers through newsboys. He was the first to use illustrations for news stories. He was the first to publish stock market prices and daily financial articles. And he was the first to employ European correspondents.

Bennett's son, James Gordon Bennett, Jr. (1841–1918), carried on the family business and in 1871, sent Henry M. Stanley to central Africa to find Dr. David Livingstone, a medical missionary who had been missing for six years.

Foreign correspondents often work alone and have little or no support staff to help them. Like other news reporters, they work under deadline pressures.

Foreign correspondents must cover conflicts of all kinds, especially war. They are often sent into unfamiliar situations in strange places. They may have to go to a battlefield to get accurate facts about the action, or they may be able to get the story from a safer location.

Foreign correspondents spend a lot of time doing research, finding leads, making appointments, and arranging travel. They make on-site observations and interview local people or those involved in the situation. Foreign correspondents often must know how to take photographs or shoot video.

After correspondents have interviewed sources or filmed an event, they write the story. Then they send it electronically to their newspaper, broadcast station, or wire service.

Many times, foreign correspondents' jobs can be lonely. They may work out of hotel rooms or have to live in remote locations where conditions are rough or primitive.

EXPLORING

○ Visit these Web sites that report international news: National Public Radio (http://www.npr.org), BBC (http://news.bbc.co.uk), CNN (http://www.cnn.com), New York Times (http://nytimes.com), International Herald Tribune (http://iht.com).

○ Work on your school newspaper as a reporter or correspondent.

○ Watch international news reports on television or the radio. Some PBS and cable stations have shows devoted entirely to international news.

○ Ask your guidance counselor to help arrange an information interview with a foreign correspondent to help you get an idea of the pros and cons of the field.

○ If you are lucky to take a trip abroad, keep a journal to record your experiences. Perhaps your school newspaper will publish your reports.

Education and Training

To prepare for a career in journalism, take high school classes in English and creative writing. You should also study foreign languages, social studies, political science, history, and geography.

To Be a Successful Foreign Correspondent, You Should . . .

○ have a love of adventure

○ be curious about how other people live

○ have good interviewing skills

○ have the courage to talk to people about uncomfortable topics

○ have excellent communication skills

○ be able to work independently

○ be able to handle deadline pressure

After high school, you must go to college and earn a bachelor's degree, preferably in journalism or English. You can also major in political science, literature, economics, or foreign language.

Earnings

Salaries for foreign correspondents depend on the publication, network, station, or other employer they work for. They also depend on the cost of living and tax structure in the country or countries where foreign correspondents are stationed. Salaries range from $50,000 to an average of about $75,000 a year. The highest-paid foreign correspondents earn $100,000 or more a year. Some employers pay for living expenses, such as the costs of a home, school for the correspondent's children, and a car.

Outlook

The number of foreign correspondent jobs has remained steady and is expected to stay about the same. It will increase if another major conflict or war (such as the Iraq War) occurs. The number of foreign correspondents is fairly low because of the high cost of keeping a foreign news bureau and the lack of interest Americans show in world news. In spite of these factors, the number of correspondents is not expected to decrease. In the near future, most job openings will arise from the need to replace those correspondents who leave their jobs.

FOR MORE INFO

The ASJA promotes the interests of freelance writers.
American Society of Journalists and Authors (ASJA)
1501 Broadway, Suite 302
New York, NY 10036-5505
Tel: 212-997-0947
http://www.asja.org

This association provides the annual publication Journalism and Mass Communication Directory, *which has information on educational programs in all areas of journalism (newspapers, magazines, television, and radio).*
Association for Education in Journalism and Mass Communication
234 Outlet Pointe Boulevard
Columbia, SC 29210-5667
Tel: 803-798-0271
http://www.aejmc.org

This organization offers internships, scholarships, and literature for college students. To read The Journalist's Road to Success: A Career Guide, *which lists schools offering degrees in news-editing, and financial aid to those interested in print journalism, visit the DJNF's Web site.*

Dow Jones Newspaper Fund (DJNF)
PO Box 300
Princeton, NJ 08543-0300
Tel: 609-452-2820
E-mail: newsfund@wsj.dowjones.com
http://djnewspaperfund.dowjones.com

For information on careers, contact
National Association of Broadcasters
1771 N Street NW
Washington, D.C. 20036-2800
Tel: 202-429-5300
E-mail: nab@nab.org
http://www.nab.org

The SPJ's Web site offers career information and information on internships and fellowships.
Society of Professional Journalists (SPJ)
Eugene S. Pulliam National Journalism Center
3909 North Meridian Street
Indianapolis, IN 46208-4011
Tel: 317-927-8000
http://www.spj.org

Visit the following Web site for comprehensive information on journalism careers, summer programs, and college journalism programs.
High School Journalism
http://www.highschooljournalism.org

Merchant Mariners

What Merchant Mariners Do

Merchant mariners manage and operate ships that carry cargo and passengers on the world's oceans and seas. They include crew-members in three departments: deck, engine, and steward. The

A Glossary of Ship Terms

aft   at, near, or toward the stern

amidships   at or near the middle of a ship

beam   the greatest width of a ship

bilge   the curved part of a ship's hull where the sides meet the bottom

bridge   a superstructure amidships; also, the place from which a ship is navigated

deck   any horizontal partition, or floor, on a ship

galley   a ship's kitchen

hatch   an opening through a deck

helm   the wheel used to steer a ship; also, the entire steering gear and the rudder

hold   a compartment below decks for storing cargo or ballast

hull   the lower body of a ship

keel   the main structural part of a ship, consisting of a metal or wooden beam extending along the bottom centerline of the vessel

poop   a superstructure at the stern

port   the left side of a vessel, looking forward

starboard   the right side of a vessel, looking forward

stem   the forward edge of the bow

stern   the back part of a vessel

deck crew handles navigation and cargo operations. The *engine crew* oversees the machinery that propels the ship. The *steward crew* is in charge of meals and living quarters.

The *captain,* or *master,* commands the entire ship and its crew. The *chief mate,* also known as the *first mate* or *chief officer,* is the captain's first assistant. He or she plans the cargo, helps with navigation, and helps keep the ship in order. The *second mate* is in charge of all the navigation equipment and charts. The *third mate* makes sure the lifeboats, firefighting equipment, and signaling equipment are in good condition.

The *radio officer* operates and repairs the radio and other electronic communications devices such as depth finders and radar. *Able seamen* get the gear ready for cargo loading or unloading and stand watch as lookouts. They also steer the vessel by handling its wheel under the direction of the *officer on watch.* The officer is usually the *quartermaster* on noncommercial ships. *Ordinary seamen* clean and wash down the ship. The *chief engineer,* with three assistants, operates the engine room and makes all machinery repairs.

EXPLORING

○ Take up any kind of boating. Become familiar with being out on the water, navigation, and safety procedures.
○ Read these and other books on shipping, ships, and the merchant marines: *America and the Sea: A Maritime History,* by Benjamin W. Labaree, William M. Fowler, Edward W. Sloan, John B. Hattendorf, and Jeffrey J. Safford (Mystic, Conn.: Mystic Seaport Museum, 1998); *A Historical Dictionary of the U.S. Merchant Marine and Shipping Industry,* by Rene De La Pedraja Toman (Westport, Conn.: Greenwood Press, 1994); *Ship,* by Brian Lavery (London, U.K.: Dorling Kindersley, 2005).
○ Visit the American Merchant Marine Museum at the U.S. Merchant Marine Academy in Kings Point, New York (http://www.usmma.edu/museum).

Education and Training

Mathematics and physics courses are good training for many merchant marine careers. In addition, computer science will prepare you for the increasing use of high technology at sea,

Which Came First?

Which came first, the U.S. Navy, U.S. Coast Guard, or U.S. Merchant Marine? The merchant marine! In June 1775, a group of patriots in Machias, Maine, used an unarmed lumber schooner to chase the fully armed British schooner *Margaretta*. In hand-to-hand combat, the patriots mortally wounded the British captain in a one-hour battle. They captured the crew's weapons, which they used to bring in additional British ships as prizes. This is considered the first sea engagement of the American Revolution and the start of the merchant marine's war role.

The U.S. Coast Guard was founded in 1790 and the U.S. Navy began in 1797.

and physical education will get you in shape for the sometimes strenuous work on a ship.

The best way to train for the many merchant marine occupations is to attend the U.S. Merchant Marine Academy in Kings Point, New York, or one of the state academies in California, Maine, Massachusetts, Michigan, New York, or Texas. At these academies, you can take either the nautical science or marine engineering program. In both programs, you learn the skills you need for the various jobs on board a ship. Upon graduation you receive a bachelor's degree and a license as either third officer or as third assistant engineer.

After you are hired for a specific job on board a merchant marine ship and get some experience, you can advance to other positions.

Earnings

Wages vary according to the worker's rank and the size of the vessel. The U.S. Department of Labor reports that 2006 earnings in water transportation occupations ranged from the minimum wage for some beginning seamen or mate positions to more than $44.65 an hour for experienced ship engineers. Median hourly earnings for ship and boat captains and operators were $25.69; ship engineers earned $26.36; and sailors and marine oilers earned $14.73. After many years of experience, captains of larger vessels, such as container ships, oil tankers, or passenger ships, may earn more than $100,000. In all merchant marine occupations, salaries increase steadily as you gain more experience.

Outlook

The employment outlook for merchant mariners during the next decade is not very good. New ships with more automated equipment can be operated with smaller crews. There is competition from foreign shippers that charge lower rates. Cargo rates and wages paid to U.S. merchant mariners are the highest in the world.

There has been a slowdown in the shipping industry, which has forced shipping companies to hire fewer merchant mariners. Many new graduates work at onshore jobs related to the maritime industry, such as with shipping companies and vessel manufacturers. Since all graduates become members of the U.S. Naval Reserve, many sign up for active duty in the navy.

FOR MORE INFO

For information on academic requirements, contact schools that offer merchant marine training, including the following:

California Maritime Academy
200 Maritime Academy Drive
Vallejo, CA 94590-8181
Tel: 707-654-1000
http://www.csum.edu

U.S. Merchant Marine Academy
300 Steamboat Road
Kings Point, NY 11024-1634
Tel: 516-773-5000
http://www.usmma.edu

For publications, statistics, and news, contact
U.S. Maritime Administration
U.S. Department of Transportation
West Building
Southeast Federal Center
1200 New Jersey Avenue SE, Second Floor
Washington, D.C. 20590
http://www.marad.dot.gov

Park Rangers

What Park Rangers Do

Park rangers protect animals and preserve forests, ponds, and other natural resources in state and national parks. They teach visitors about the park by giving lectures and tours. They also make sure rules and regulations are followed to maintain a safe environment for visitors and wildlife. The National Park Service is one of the major employers of park rangers. In addition, park rangers work for other federal land and resource management agencies and similar state and local agencies.

One of the most important responsibilities park rangers have is safety. Rangers often require visitors to register at park offices so they will know when the visitors are expected to

The Most Popular National Parks, 2006

1. Great Smoky Mountains (North Carolina, Tennessee), http://www.nps.gov/grsm
2. Grand Canyon (Arizona), http://www.nps.gov/grca
3. Yosemite (California), http://www.nps.gov/yose
4. Yellowstone (Idaho, Montana, Wyoming), http://www.nps.gov/yell
5. Olympic (Washington), http://www.nps.gov/olym
6. Rocky Mountain (Colorado), http://www.nps.gov/romo
7. Zion (Utah), http://www.nps.gov/zion
8. Cuyahoga Valley (Ohio), http://www.nps.gov/cuva
9. Grand Teton (Wyoming), http://www.nps.gov/grte
10. Acadia (Maine), http://www.nps.gov/acad

Source: National Park Service

return from a hike or other activity. Rangers are trained in first aid and, if there is an accident, they may have to help visitors who have been injured. Rangers carefully mark hiking trails and other areas to lessen the risk of injuries for visitors and to protect plants and animals.

Rangers help visitors enjoy and learn about parks. They give lectures and provide guided tours of the park, explaining why certain plants and animals live there. They teach visitors about the rocks and soil in the area and point out important historical sites.

Research and conservation efforts are also a big part of a park ranger's responsibilities. Park rangers study wildlife behavior by tagging and following certain animals. They may investigate sources of pollution that come from outside the park. Then they develop plans to help reduce pollution to make the park a better place for plants, animals, and visitors.

Rangers also do bookkeeping and other paperwork. They issue permits to visitors and keep track of how many people use the park. They also plan recreational activities and decide how to spend the money budgeted to the park.

Education and Training

In high school, take courses in earth science, biology, mathematics, history,

EXPLORING

○ Read as much as you can about local, state, and national parks. The National Park Service's Web site, http://www.nps.gov, is a great place to start.

○ Get to know your local wildlife. What kind of insects, birds, fish, and other animals live in your area? Your librarian or science teacher will be able to help you find books that identify local flora and fauna.

○ You can gain valuable hands-on experience by getting involved in the Volunteers-in-Parks (VIP) program, which is sponsored by the National Park Service. Park volunteers help park employees in many ways, including answering phone calls, welcoming visitors, maintaining trails, building fences, painting buildings, and picking up litter. For more information, visit http://www.nps.gov/volunteer.

○ You also may be able to volunteer at state, county, or local parks. Universities and conservation organizations often have volunteer groups that work on research activities, studies, and rehabilitation efforts.

To Be a Successful Park Ranger, You Should . . .

○ know about protecting plants and animals

○ be good at explaining the natural environment

○ enjoy working outdoors

○ have a pleasant personality

○ be able to work with many different kinds of people

○ be in good physical shape

○ be able to enforce park rules and regulations

English, and speech. Any classes or activities that deal with plant and animal life, the weather, geography, and interacting with others will be helpful.

Park rangers usually have bachelor's degrees in natural resource or recreational resource management. A degree in many other fields, such as biology or ecology, is also acceptable. Classes in forestry, geology, outdoor management, history, geography, behavioral sciences, and botany are helpful. Without a degree, you need at least three years of experience

Our National Parks

Congress began the National Park System in 1872 when Yellowstone National Park was created. The National Park Service, a bureau of the U.S. Department of the Interior, was created in 1916 to preserve, protect, and manage the national, cultural, historical, and recreational areas of the National Park System. At that time, the entire park system occupied less than one million acres. Today, the country's national parks cover more than 84 million acres of mountains, plains, deserts, swamps, historic sites, lakeshores, forests, rivers, battlefields, memorials, archaeological properties, and recreation areas.

working in parks or conservation. Rangers also receive on-the-job training.

Earnings

In 2007, new rangers in the National Park Service earned between \$25,623 and \$33,309 annually. Rangers with some experience earned between \$31,740 and \$41,262. The most experienced rangers who supervise other workers earn more than \$80,000 a year. The government may provide housing to rangers who work in remote areas.

Rangers in state parks work for the state government. According to the National Association of State Park Directors,

FOR MORE INFO

For information about state parks and employment opportunities, contact
National Association of State Park Directors
8829 Woodyhill Road
Raleigh, NC 27613-1134
Tel: 919-676-8365
E-mail: NASPD@nc.rr.com
http://www.naspd.org

For detailed information about careers with the National Park Service, contact
National Park Service
U.S. Department of the Interior
1849 C Street NW
Washington, D.C. 20240-0002
Tel: 202-208-6843
http://www.nps.gov

For general career information, contact the following organizations:
National Parks Conservation Association

1300 19th Street NW, Suite 300
Washington, D.C. 20036-1628
Tel: 800-628-7275
E-mail: npca@npca.org
http://www.npca.org

National Recreation and Park Association
22377 Belmont Ridge Road
Ashburn, VA 20148-4501
Tel: 703-858-0784
http://www.nrpa.org

For information on student volunteer activities and programs, contact
Student Conservation Association
689 River Road
PO Box 550
Charlestown, NH 03603-0550
Tel: 603-543-1700
E-mail: ask-us@sca-inc.org
http://www.thesca.org

rangers employed by state parks had average starting salaries of $24,611 in 2004.

Outlook

The number of people who want to become park rangers has always been far greater than the number of positions available. The National Park Service has reported that as many as 100 people apply for each job opening. This trend should continue into the future, and because of this stiff competition for positions, the job outlook is expected to change little. As a result, those interested in the field should attain the greatest number and widest variety of applicable skills possible. They may wish to study subjects they can use in other fields, such as forestry, land management, conservation, wildlife management, history, and natural sciences.

Pilots

What Pilots Do

Airplane pilots operate aircraft. They transport passengers, freight, and mail and perform other commercial duties. The best-known pilots are *commercial airline pilots,* who fly for large airlines. They are in command of their crew, the plane, and the passengers during the time the plane is in motion on the runway and in the air.

Pilots first check the weather, the flight conditions, and the flight plan, which is approved by the Federal Aviation Administration (FAA) and air traffic control personnel. On board a plane the pilot and *copilot,* who assists the pilot, test the instruments, controls, and electronic and mechanical systems. The pilot then gets orders from a dispatcher and taxis the plane (drives it at a slow speed along the ground) to a runway. There the pilot asks for permission to take off.

Much of the time the plane is in the air it is being flown using an electronic device called an automatic pilot. The pilot and copilot continue to make radio reports to the ground,

The First Flight

The age of modern aviation began with the famous flight of Orville and Wilbur Wright's heavier-than-air machine on December 17, 1903. On that day, the Wright brothers flew their machine four times and became the first airplane pilots. In the early days of aviation, the pilot's job was quite different from that of today's pilots. When Orville Wright flew that first plane, he was lying on his stomach in the middle of the bottom wing of the plane. There was a strap across his hips, and to turn the plane, he had to tilt his hips from side to side.

EXPLORING

○ Read books and magazines about aviation and pilot careers.

○ Join a high school aviation club.

○ Learn to operate a ham radio. One of the qualifications for commercial flying is ham radio operation. There are many clubs that hold meetings and classes to teach the basic skills of radio operation and prepare you for your ham radio license test. You will find more information by contacting the American Radio Relay League, 225 Main Street, Newington, CT 06111-1494, 860-594-0200, http://www.arrl.org.

○ At 16 years of age, you may start taking flying lessons.

checking altitude, speed, weather conditions, and other details. Before landing, the pilot rechecks the landing gear and requests landing clearance from air traffic controllers. When weather conditions are poor and the crew cannot see the runway, the captain may have to land the plane guided only by the plane's landing instruments.

There are many other kinds of pilots. *Agricultural pilots* spray crops to control insects and weeds, and to fertilize. These pilots are experts at flying but they must also understand the work of the farmers. *Helicopter pilots* transport passengers from jet airports to city centers. Helicopters are also used in emergency medical care, rescue service, sightseeing, conservation service, traffic reporting, and aerial photography.

Education and Training

All aspiring pilots must complete high school. A college-preparatory curriculum is recommended because pilots need to have at least some college education. Science and mathematics are two important subjects, and you should also take advantage of any computer courses offered. You can start pursuing your pilot's license while in high school.

Many airlines require that their trainees be college graduates. You will need to study meteorology, algebra, geometry, and mechanical drawing.

Pilots must meet strict training requirements, especially to work for commercial airlines. After flight instruction, you must

What Do Helicopter Pilots Do?

Helicopter pilots work in medical evacuation, police and firefighting work, forestry, construction, communications, agriculture, and offshore oil exploration. They carry workers and supplies to oil rigs, rescue stranded flood victims, lift heavy materials to work sites, fly patients from one hospital to another, or give news and traffic updates for the media. Helicopter pilots who do police work are sometimes law enforcement officers as well. Their work includes traffic regulation and survey, vehicle pursuits, surveillance, patrol, and search.

During flight, helicopter pilots monitor dials and gauges to make sure the aircraft is working properly. They watch for changes in pressure, fuel, and temperature. They navigate using landmarks, compasses, maps, and radio equipment.

In addition to flying, helicopter pilots keep records of their aircraft's engine performance and file flight plans. Before and after flying, they check the aircraft for problems and may even do repairs and general upkeep on the craft if they are licensed to do so.

Education and Training: Some helicopter pilots receive training in flying schools where, in addition to flight training, they study the theory of flying, weather, radio, navigation, and FAA regulations. Many helicopter pilots learn to fly as officers in the army. A military pilot must pass the FAA military competency exam to become licensed as a commercial helicopter pilot.

Earnings: Helicopter pilots earned salaries that ranged from less than $55,205 to $112,364 or more in 2007, according to Salary.com.

Outlook: The future of the helicopter industry is fair to good, growing by about 5 percent a year. Helicopters are being used more and more by police, fire, and rescue departments and in other fields and industries.

pass a written exam and accumulate 250 hours of flying time. Then you can apply for a commercial airline pilot's license. To receive this license, you must pass a physical exam and a written exam given by the FAA. Then you can apply for a copilot's position with an airline. Airlines have their own requirements, which often include up to 1,500 hours of flight time.

FOR MORE INFO

To read Looking for a Career Where the Sky Is the Limit?, *visit the ALPA's Web site.*
Air Line Pilots Association (ALPA)
1625 Massachusetts Avenue NW
Washington, D.C. 20036-2212
Tel: 703-689-2270
http://www.alpa.org

To read The Airline Handbook, *visit the ATAA's Web site.*
Air Transport Association of America (ATAA)
1301 Pennsylvania Avenue NW, Suite 1100
Washington, D.C. 20004-1738
Tel: 202-626-4000
E-mail: ata@airlines.org
http://www.airlines.org

For information on careers, contact
Federal Aviation Administration
800 Independence Avenue SW, Room 810
Washington, D.C. 20591
Tel: 866-835-5322
http://www.faa.gov

Earnings

The U.S. Department of Labor reports that median annual earnings of airline pilots, copilots, and flight engineers were $141,090 in 2006. The lowest 10 percent earned less than $50,470. Commercial pilots had median annual earnings of $57,480 in 2006. Salaries ranged from less than $28,450 to more than $115,220.

Outlook

Employment for pilots will grow about as fast as the average. There is a lot of competition for pilot jobs. The high pay, prestige, and travel benefits make this a popular career choice for a growing number of people.

Opportunities will be best at regional airlines and low-fare carriers, which have experienced faster growth than the major airlines. Pilots who fly for air cargo carriers will also have good opportunities as these companies receive more shipping business as a result of security restrictions on the shipping of freight via passenger airlines.

Employment opportunities for experienced agricultural pilots are expected to continue into the future, but these opportunities depend on farmers' needs.

Police Officers

What Police Officers Do

Police officers protect the lives and property of citizens by upholding and enforcing laws. Police officers preserve the peace, prevent criminal acts, and arrest people who break the law.

Some officers are assigned to traffic duties. They direct traffic during busy times of the day and ticket motorists who break traffic laws. Other police officers are assigned to patrol duties. These officers work in public places, such as in parks or on the streets, to make sure no one violates the law. They may patrol on foot, in squad cars, on bicycles, on motorcycles, or on horseback. They also look out for stolen cars, missing children, and persons wanted by law enforcement agencies.

Police officers also help in emergency situations. They administer first aid to accident victims, see that sick or injured

A police officer issues a ticket to a woman he caught speeding. (Jeff Greenberg, The Image Works)

Words to Learn

adam codes radio codes used to describe types of calls; for example, A1 means arrest, A20 means assistance rendered, and A63 means pursuit

probable cause information uncovered by officers that gives them a reason to arrest, search, or stop and detain a person

reasonable suspicion the reasons an officer believes a person should be stopped and detained

surveillance following, observing, or listening to people for the purpose of obtaining information about criminal activities

people are rushed to hospitals, and help firefighters by controlling crowds and rerouting traffic. Police officers also prevent or break up violent disturbances.

Most police officers are trained to use firearms and carry guns. Police in special divisions, such as chemical analysis and handwriting and fingerprint identification, have special training. Officers often testify in court regarding the cases they

It's a Fact

Sir Robert Peel established the first modern, nonmilitary police force in 1829 in London, England. The British police became known as bobbies after Sir Robert's name. The police force in New York City was established in 1844. These new police officers wore uniforms, worked 24 hours a day, and often carried guns as they patrolled the streets. On the American frontier, laws were often enforced by volunteer police officers. Many areas of the West were guarded by a sheriff and the sheriff's deputies. An effort to establish a statewide police force resulted in the creation of the Texas Rangers in 1835. In 1905, Pennsylvania formed the first official state police department. Soon, almost every state had a state police department as well as police units that worked for individual cities or towns.

handle. Police also have to complete accurate and thorough records of their cases.

Education and Training

The requirements for becoming a police officer are strict. You must pass many tests to prove you are qualified to be a police officer. These tests include written exams and tests of physical strength, dexterity, and endurance. Medical histories are checked carefully to find any medical condition that might hinder your work. There are background checks to make sure you are a U.S. citizen and have no history of criminal activity or convictions.

Most police departments require you to have at least a high school diploma. In some cases, you also need college training. Many colleges and junior colleges now offer programs in law enforcement, police work, and police administration.

After you are accepted by a police force, you start special training. It may last from three to six months or longer. Training usually includes classroom work in local, state, and federal laws; physical fitness training; firearm instruction; and legal procedures for enforcing the law.

EXPLORING

○ Play games and make up exercises to test your memory and powers of observation. For example, you might play a video (or DVD) you have never seen before. Forward the tape to a random spot and play it for 30 seconds. Stop the video and write down everything you observed. Describe the setting, the people, their clothing, what they said, background noise, and so on. Then replay the video and check your accuracy. Try this with friends and compare notes.

○ Many police departments have programs for kids. Look for educational events that teach you about street safety, Internet safety, or self-defense.

○ Participate in police-sponsored sports events or social activities. Doing so will give you a chance to meet and talk with police officers.

Earnings

According to the U.S. Department of Labor, police officers earned an annual average salary of $47,460 in 2006. The

FOR MORE INFO

For information on careers in policing, check out this Web site:

International Police Association
http://www.ipa-usa.org

The National Association of Police Organizations is a coalition of police unions and associations that work to advance the interests of law enforcement officers through legislation, political action, and education.

National Association of Police Organizations
317 South Patrick Street
Alexandria, VA 22314-3501
Tel: 703-549-0775
E-mail: info@napo.org
http://www.napo.org

lowest 10 percent earned less than $27,310 a year, while the highest 10 percent earned $72,450 or more annually. Police officers in supervisory positions earned median salaries of $69,310 a year in 2006, with a low of less than $41,260 and a high of more than $104,410.

Salaries for police officers range widely based on location. Police departments in the West and North generally pay more than those in the South.

Outlook

Employment for police officers will increase about as fast as the average, but there is a lot of competition for openings. This occupation has a very low turnover rate. However, new positions will open as officers retire, leave the force, or move into higher positions. Police officers retire early compared to other occupations. Many retire while in their forties or fifties and then pursue second careers.

In the past 10 years, private security firms have taken over some police activities, such as patrolling airports and other public places. Some private companies even provide police forces for entire cities. Many companies and universities also operate their own police forces.

Private Investigators

What Private Investigators Do

Private investigators, or *private detectives,* investigate crimes, help find missing persons, serve as bodyguards to important people, and collect information for trials and other legal proceedings. They do a lot of library and Internet research, fact checking, and telephone interviews.

Private investigators do many of the same things as police officers. They gather clues from accidents, observe suspects, and check people's personal histories to learn more about their backgrounds. There are two important differences between police officers and investigators: investigators do not have to follow the same legal procedures when they interview suspects and collect evidence, and investigators cannot make arrests. Private detectives sometimes work with police officers to solve crimes.

Private investigators usually work for agencies. Clients come to these agencies with specific problems. For example, a business owner might hire an investigator to prevent shoplifting, vandalism, or another type of business crime. Investigators may be asked to look into insurance claims to make sure that people who are claiming property damage have actually had property destroyed or stolen. In all cases, investigators report to their clients on the details of their case.

Popular Specialties

Here are the some of the most popular private investigation specialties:

- insurance claims investigation
- background checks
- location of missing persons
- surveillance
- executive protection
- countermeasures
- fraud investigation
- criminal investigations
- accident investigations

EXPLORING

○ Ask your librarian to help you find books and magazines on detectives.

○ There are few means of exploring the field of detective work, and actual experience in the field prior to employment is unlikely. If you are interested in becoming a private investigator, you should talk with your school guidance counselor, your local police department, local private detective agencies, a private investigation school, or a college or university offering police science, criminal justice, or law enforcement courses.

○ Practice your detective skills by playing board games, such as 221b Baker Street, Clue, 13 Dead End Drive, Murder She Wrote, and Scotland Yard. Additionally, there are many computer games that test your mystery- and puzzle-solving skills.

These reports are usually written and then explained orally.

A private investigator's work can lead to the recovery of stolen valuables, the arrest of a criminal, or the uncovering of a spy operation. But for every success there are many hours of searching for clues. Investigations can be dangerous. Investigators may have to go into rough neighborhoods late at night looking for witnesses, or suspects may threaten them. Most of the work, however, is safe.

Education and Training

Many people become investigators after working as police officers. There are several detective training programs that teach you to locate missing persons, interview people, check public records, lift fingerprints, pick locks, and operate cameras and other surveillance equipment. These programs are usually several months long. Students then receive on-the-job training at a detective agency before they become investigators. Most programs only accept high school graduates. There are also many community colleges and universities that offer degree programs in criminal justice or a related field.

Most states require private investigators to take a licensing test. Those who carry a gun usually have to pass an examination to show they know how to use a firearm. Some states require law enforcement experience or an apprenticeship period with an experienced investigator before they can get a license.

Earnings

Median annual earnings of salaried private detectives and investigators were $33,750 in 2006, according to the U.S. Department of Labor. The lowest 10 percent earned less than $19,720, and the highest 10 percent earned more than $64,380. Self-employed investigators can earn from $50 to $150 or more an hour.

Trends in Private Investigation

Countermeasures

U.S. businesses are losing billions of dollars a year through theft of trade secrets and illegal eavesdropping. Business and industry are hiring private investigators to take countermeasures against these crimes. (For example, they find hidden surveillance equipment.)

Digital Data Recovery and Computer Crime

More and more data is being stored on computers instead of on paper. As a result, more private investigators are specializing in investigating computer crime and recovering electronic data.

Domestic Investigations

Divorce investigation has been the primary work for many private investigation agencies since the 1950s. It is still a major trend today. Divorce investigations can involve surveillance and activities checks, child custody and child abuse issues, as well as discovering hidden assets.

Nursing Homes

More private investigators are working with attorneys to uncover abuse in nursing homes.

Premises Liability

Attorneys and private investigators are working together to investigate premises liability, specifically in the area of inadequate security (landlords and businesses fail to provide adequate security).

PIs Focus on Kids

A number of private investigation firms now specialize in children's cases. Divorces, the increasing use of daily child care, and the awareness of child abuse have led to this specialization, which focuses on these areas:

- ○ background checks for child care workers
- ○ background checks on nannies
- ○ rental of temporary video camera equipment
- ○ child abuse investigation

FOR MORE INFO

For industry information, contact
National Association of Investigative Specialists
PO Box 82148
Austin, TX 78708-2148
Tel: 512-719-3595
http://www.pimall.com/nais/nais.j.html

For information on certification, contact
National Association of Legal Investigators
235 North Pine Street
Lansing, MI 48933-1021
Tel: 866-520-6254
http://www.nalionline.org

Outlook

Employment for investigators is expected to grow faster than the average. Many job openings are created by those who leave the profession because of the long working hours and possible danger. The use of private investigators by insurance firms, restaurants, hotels, and other businesses is on the rise. An area of especially fast growth is the investigation of different kinds of computer fraud.

Reporters

What Reporters Do

Reporters gather information and report the news for radio, television, magazines, newspapers, and Web sites. They cover stories on local, national, or international events. Correspondents cover stories from a specific area. For example, each national network station has a White House correspondent, a congressional correspondent, and a Pentagon (the headquarters of the U.S. Department of Defense) correspondent.

Reporters and correspondents gather all the information they need to write or broadcast clear and accurate news stories. They interview people, research the facts and history behind a story, observe important events, and then write the story. News stories may be a one-day item, such as a power failure or weather-related piece. Or they may cover a period of days or weeks, on subjects such as trials, investigations, major disasters, and government issues.

To gather information, reporters research and take notes and record or videotape interviews with sources. Before reporters start putting together their stories, they discuss the subject matter with an *editor* or a *producer.* Editors and producers decide what news will be covered each day. They determine how long a story should be and how much importance to give it.

Profile of Daily Newspaper Subscribers, 2006

- ○ 89 percent were white; 8 percent were African American; 7 percent were Hispanic; and 1 percent were Asian
- ○ 82 percent were homeowners
- ○ 64 percent were 45 years of age and older
- ○ 53 percent of subscribers were women
- ○ 51 percent earned $50,000 or more annually
- ○ 25 percent had a bachelor's degree or higher

Source: 2006 Newspaper Association of America Engagement Custom Recontact Study

Sometimes they decide to hold the story for a while or not to run it at all.

Reporters then organize the information and write a concise, informative story. Reporters and correspondents who are far from their editorial office may phone, e-mail, or fax in their stories. Television reporters may broadcast from the scene of a story.

Because of continual deadline pressure, a reporter's life is hectic. Stories for nightly news broadcasts have to be in and reviewed by the producer before airtime. Newspaper articles must be filed long before the first edition is printed, usually in the very early hours of the morning. If a major news story takes place, reporters may have to work 18 or 20 hours without a break.

Some correspondents are assigned to cover dangerous areas. War stories are frequently filed from the country where the war is taking place. Reporters who cover riots, floods, major disasters, and other stories must be able to work in difficult, dangerous, and upsetting situations.

The All-important Interview

Good reporters are usually good interviewers. They interview experts to get the details of a story. For example, they might talk to an oncologist (a physician who specializes in caring for people with cancer) about a new cancer treatment. Reporters interview eyewitnesses, such as customers who saw a bank robber, or people who lived through a hurricane. They interview people to get their opinions on news events, such as citizens who might be affected by the construction of a superhighway through their neighborhood. Interviews are important for getting the facts, supporting the facts, and getting various sides of the story.

Take a look at your local newspaper and watch television news reports. How many stories use interviews? What questions did the reporters ask? Did the interviews supply important information? Would the story have been as good without the interviews?

Education and Training

You can begin to prepare for a career as a reporter in high school. Take courses in English, writing, history, typing, and computer science. After high school, you should go to college and earn a bachelor's degree. Your degree can be in journalism or liberal arts. Master's degrees are becoming more important for journalists, particularly for teachers and specialists.

Earnings

According to the U.S. Department of Labor, the median salary for reporters and correspondents was $33,470 in 2006. The lowest paid 10 percent of these workers earned $19,180 or less per year, while the highest paid

EXPLORING

○ Read your local newspaper regularly. Follow the work of one or two reporters who cover a topic that interests you.
○ Talk to reporters and editors at local newspapers and radio and TV stations or interview the admissions counselor at the school of journalism closest to your home. Ask a teacher or guidance counselor to help you arrange the interviews.
○ Work on your school newspaper or on a church, synagogue, or mosque newsletter.

10 percent made $73,880 or more annually. Mean annual earnings for reporters employed in newspaper, book, and directory publishing were $38,620; in Internet publishing, $42,690; and in radio and television, $50,730.

Outlook

Employment for reporters and correspondents is expected to grow more slowly than the average. In television news, cutbacks have affected most large stations and all of the networks. While the number of self-employed reporters is expected to grow, newspaper jobs are expected to decrease because of mergers, consolidations, and closures in the newspaper industry. Newspapers in large cities usually hire reporters with some experience, so beginning journalists will find more jobs in small towns or at smaller publications and stations. Some major daily newspapers offer a limited number of one-year, full-time internships, with no guarantee that they will be kept on afterward.

FOR MORE INFO

This association produces the annual publication Journalism and Mass Communication Directory, *which has information on educational programs in all areas of journalism.*

Association for Education in Journalism and Mass Communication
234 Outlet Pointe Boulevard
Columbia, SC 29210-5667
Tel: 803-798-0271
http://www.aejmc.edu

This organization offers internships, scholarships, and literature for college students.

Dow Jones Newspaper Fund (DJNF)
PO Box 300
Princeton, NJ 08543-0300
Tel: 609-452-2820
E-mail: newsfund@wsj.dowjones.com
http://djnewspaperfund.dowjones.com

For information on careers in newspapers, contact

Newspaper Association of America
4401 Wilson Boulevard, Suite 900
Arlington, VA 22203-1867
Tel: 571-366-1000
E-mail: IRC@naa.org
http://www.naa.org

Visit the following Web site for comprehensive information on journalism careers, summer programs, and college journalism programs.

High School Journalism
http://www.highschooljournalism.org

Secret Service Special Agents

What Secret Service Special Agents Do

Secret Service special agents protect U.S. leaders or foreign leaders who are visiting the United States. Special agents also investigate the counterfeiting of U.S. currency and other financial crimes. Special agents can carry and use firearms, execute warrants, and make arrests.

Special agents plan the best ways to guard the people they are assigned to protect. For example, an advance team of special agents surveys the places a protectee (see "Words to Learn") is scheduled to visit. They identify hospitals and exit routes and work closely with local police, fire, and rescue units to develop a protection plan. They set up a command post as the communication center for protective activities. Before the

Words to Learn

choke point a potential ambush site—like a bridge—where a protectee or motorcade may be more vulnerable to attack

protectee a person—usually a political leader of the United States or a foreign dignitary—that the Secret Service is responsible for protecting; protectees may also include the spouse or family of the primary protectee

protective bubble a 360-degree boundary of safety that the Secret Service maintains around each of its protectees; special agents try to prevent dangers from penetrating the bubble

Special agents monitor the crowd for suspicious activity as President Bush leaves a public function. (Bob Daemmrich, The Image Works)

protectee arrives, a *lead advance agent* coordinates all law enforcement representatives participating in the visit. He or she tells agents where they will be posted and notifies them about any special concerns. Just before the arrival of the protectee, agents set up checkpoints and limit access to secure the area. After the visit, special agents analyze every step of the operation, record unusual incidents, and suggest improvements for the future.

Then and Now

The Secret Service was established in 1865 to stop the counterfeiting of U.S. currency. After the assassination of President William McKinley in 1901, the Secret Service was directed by Congress to protect the president of the United States. Today it is the Secret Service's responsibility to protect the following people:

○ the president and vice president (also president-elect and vice president–elect) and their immediate families

○ former presidents and their spouses for 10 years after the president leaves office (spouses lose protection if they remarry)

○ children of former presidents until they are 16 years old

○ visiting heads of foreign states or governments and their spouses traveling with them, along with other distinguished foreign visitors to the United States and their spouses traveling with them

○ official representatives of the United States who are performing special missions abroad

○ major presidential and vice-presidential candidates and, within 120 days of the general presidential election, their spouses

○ other individuals as designated per Executive Order of the president and National Special Security Events, when designated as such by the secretary of the Department of Homeland Security

When secret service special agents are not working on a protective assignment, they work on crime investigations. For example, they investigate threats made to protectees and cases of counterfeit currency, forgery, and financial crimes.

Education and Training

Computer and foreign language classes are good preparation for a career in the Secret Service, as are government and English classes.

After high school there are several ways to qualify for entry into the Secret Service. You can earn a four-year degree from a college or university. You can work for at least three years in a criminal investigative or law enforcement field. Or a combination of education and experience can also qualify you.

EXPLORING
- Visit the Student Q&A page on the Secret Service Web site at http://www.secretservice.gov/kids_faq.shtml.
- The Secret Service offers the Stay-In-School Program for high school students. The program allows students who meet financial eligibility guidelines to earn money by working for the agency part time, usually in a clerical job. Contact the Secret Service (http://www.secretservice.gov) for more information.

All newly hired agents go through nine weeks of training at the Federal Law Enforcement Training Center in Glynco, Georgia. This is followed by 11 weeks of specialized training at the Secret Service's Training Academy in Beltsville, Maryland.

Special agents must be U.S. citizens; be at least 21 at the time of appointment; have uncorrected vision no worse than 20/60 in each eye, correctable to 20/20 in each eye; pass an examination; and undergo a complete background investigation, including in-depth interviews, drug screening, medical examination, and polygraph examination.

Earnings

Agents usually start at the GS-5, GS-7, or GS-9 grade levels (pay scales established by the federal government), which

FOR MORE INFO

Your local Secret Service field office or its headquarters, can provide more information on becoming a special agent. If you are inquiring about the Stay-In-School program, mark the envelope "Attention: Stay-In-School Program."

U.S. Secret Service
245 Murray Drive SW, Building 410
Washington, D.C. 20223-0008
Tel: 202-406-5708
http://www.secretservice.gov

were $25,623, $31,740, and $38,824 in 2007, respectively. Salaries may be slightly higher in some areas with high costs of living. Agents automatically advance by two pay grades each year, until they reach the GS-12 level, which was $56,301 in 2007. Agents must compete for positions above the GS-12 level; however, the majority of agents become a GS-13—$66,951 in 2007—in their career.

Outlook

Compared to other federal law enforcement agencies, the Secret Service is small. It employs about 6,400 people, 3,200 of whom are special agents. As a result, the number of agents it hires each year is limited. Individuals with prior experience in law enforcement and advanced degrees will have the best employment prospects.

Spies

What Spies Do

Spies, also called *intelligence officers,* work for the U.S. government to gather information about the governments of foreign countries. This information, called intelligence, is one of the tools the U.S. government uses to help make decisions about its own military, economic, and political policies. Intelligence may include political, economic, military, scientific, technical, geographic, and other types of information, both public and secret.

There are two types of intelligence officers, *case officers* and *analysts.* Case officers, also called *operators,* are most often involved in the colorful and dangerous sorts of activities shown in the movies. They collect intelligence, usually in foreign countries. They contact people who supply them with the valuable information they need. Analysts are more likely to be stationed in an office in Washington, D.C., although some also work abroad. They interpret and analyze data they have received from case officers and other sources. Technical analysts gather data from satellites. *Cryptographic technicians* are experts at encoding, decoding, and sending secret messages.

There are three categories of intelligence operations: strategic, tactical, and

Intelligence Facts

Intelligence is information gathered by intelligence officers to help the U.S. government and its policy makers. There are several different kinds of intelligence:

- ○ *Current intelligence* is information about day-to-day events.
- ○ *Estimative intelligence* considers what might be or what might happen.
- ○ *Research intelligence* is an in-depth study of an issue.
- ○ *Scientific and technical intelligence* is information on foreign technologies.
- ○ *Warning intelligence* gives notice to policy makers that something urgent might happen that may require their immediate attention.

EXPLORING

Here are some books, movies, and a Web site to explore.

Books

○ *In the Line of Fire: Eight Women War Spies,* by George Sullivan (New York: Scholastic, 1996)

○ *Spies and Traitors,* by Stewart Ross (London, U.K.: Aladdin/Watts, 1995)

○ *The Spy Who Came In from the Sea,* by Peggy Nolan (Sarasota, Fla.: Pineapple Press, 2001)

Movies

○ *Above Suspicion,* directed by Richard Thorpe (1943)

○ *The Good Shepherd,* directed by Robert DeNiro (2006)

○ *The 39 Steps,* directed by Alfred Hitchcock (1935)

○ *Tinker, Tailor, Soldier, Spy,* directed by John Irvin (1980)

Web Site

○ CIA Kids' Page: https://www.cia.gov/kids-page/index.html

counterintelligence. People working in strategic intelligence keep track of world events, watch foreign leaders very carefully, and study a foreign country's politics, economy, people, military status, and any scientific advances it may be making. Tactical intelligence–gathering involves collecting the same kind of information, but in combat areas and risky political settings abroad. Counterintelligence officers protect U.S. secrets, institutions, and intelligence activities. They identify and prevent enemy operations that might hurt the United States, its citizens, or its allies. Such enemy plots include worldwide terrorism and drug trafficking.

Education and Training

If you are interested in becoming a spy, you can begin preparing in high school by taking courses in English, history, government, journalism, geography, social studies, and foreign languages. You should develop your writing and computer skills as well. Students with the highest grades have the best possibilities for finding employment as spies.

All of the federal intelligence services are looking for people of high moral character, with excellent academic records and sincere patriotic commitment. Applicants must be U.S. citizens and at least 21 years old. You must earn a bachelor's degree, and an advanced degree for some positions. Specialized skills,

Famous Women Spies

○ Lydia Barrington Darragh spied on the British during the American Revolution and informed American officers.

○ Sarah Bradlee Fulton, called the "mother of the Boston Tea Party" delivered messages across enemy lines.

○ Belle Boyd spied for the Confederacy and carried letters and papers across enemy lines during the Civil War.

○ Elizabeth Van Lew spied for the North during the Civil War, setting up a network of couriers and inventing a code.

○ Edith Cavell, a nurse from England, helped British, French, and Belgian soldiers escape from behind German lines during WW I.

○ Virginia Hall worked for the French as an agent and later for America's OSS (Office of Strategic Services) during WW II, successfully evading the Nazis.

computer knowledge, and fluency in foreign languages are also important.

Earnings

The starting salary for intelligence officers with a bachelor's degree ranges from $31,740 to $46,974. A candidate with an advanced degree in engineering or a physical science may start as high as $62,000. Those with experience and knowledge of a foreign language also earn higher salaries. Those in top management earn from $74,000 to $114,000 a year. Officers who work abroad receive free housing and allowances and benefits. Those employed in secret or hazardous operations also receive higher pay.

FOR MORE INFO

For information on the intelligence community, contact
Association For Intelligence Officers
6723 Whittier Avenue, Suite 303A
McLean, VA 22101-4533
Tel: 703-790-0320
E-mail: afio@afio.com
http://www.afio.com

For information on career paths, contact
Central Intelligence Agency
Office of Public Affairs
Washington, D.C. 20505
Tel: 703-482-0623
http://www.cia.gov/employment

For information on intelligence careers, contact the following government agencies:
Defense Intelligence Agency
http://www.dia.mil/employment

Federal Bureau of Investigation
http://www.fbijobs.gov

National Security Agency
http://www.nsa.gov/careers/index.cfm

U.S. Department of Homeland Security
http://www.dhs.gov/xabout/careers

U.S. Department of State
http://www.careers.state.gov

Outlook

While the fall of Communism in Eastern Europe and in the former Soviet republics greatly reduced the number and intensity of intelligence operations in these countries, other parts of the world now demand more urgent attention from all agencies. For this reason, the outlook for intelligence jobs remains good, and new officers will be hired every year. There are ongoing threats of terrorism in other parts of the world, so the need for intelligence activities will remain high. Intelligence agencies are concerned with the spread of nuclear, chemical, and biological weapons. Intelligence has become one of the world's largest industries. In the United States alone, it is supported by a multibillion-dollar annual budget.

Stunt Performers

What Stunt Performers Do

Stunt performers work on film and television scenes that are risky and dangerous. They act out car crashes and chases, fist and sword fights, and falls from cars, motorcycles, horses, and buildings. They perform airplane and helicopter gags, ride through river rapids, and face wild animals. Some stunt performers specialize in one type of stunt.

There are two general types of stunt roles: *double* and *nondescript.* The first requires a stunt performer to double, or take the place of a star actor in a dangerous scene. As a double, the stunt performer must portray the character in the same way as the star actor. In a nondescript role, the stunt performer does not stand in for another actor, but plays an incidental character in a dangerous scene. An example of a nondescript role is a driver in a freeway chase scene. Stunt performers rarely have speaking parts.

The idea for a stunt usually begins with the screenwriter. Once the stunts are written into the script, it is the job of the director to decide how they will appear on the screen. Directors, especially of large, action-filled movies, often seek the help of a *stunt coordinator.* A stunt coordinator can quickly determine if a stunt is possible and what is the best and safest way to perform it. The stunt coordinator

Stunt Specialties

Here are some of the skills stunt performers learn in training programs at The United Stuntmen's Association (See "For More Info"):

- ○ precision driving
- ○ weaponry
- ○ unarmed combat
- ○ horse work
- ○ fire burns
- ○ stair falls
- ○ climbing and repelling
- ○ martial arts
- ○ high falls

Women Daredevils

The stunts of these women daredevils in the nineteenth century drew as many spectators as those of the men.

○ Signora Josephine Girardelli was known as the "fire-proof lady." She earned that title by holding boiling oil in her mouth and hands and performing other feats of stamina.

○ Bess Houdini assisted her husband Harry in many famous tricks, including one that ended with her tied up and sealed in a trunk.

○ May Wirth was a talented equestrian, known as "The Wonder Rider of the World" for her somersaults and other stunts while riding a rushing horse.

○ Even amateurs got into the act—Annie Taylor, a 63-year-old Michigan schoolteacher, became the first person to go over Niagara Falls in a barrel.

plans the stunt, oversees the setup and construction of special sets and materials, and either hires or recommends the most qualified stunt performer.

Although a stunt may last only a few seconds on film, preparations for the stunt can take several hours or even days. Stunt performers work with props, makeup, wardrobe, and set design departments. They also work closely with the special effects team. A carefully planned stunt can often be completed in just one take. It is more common for the stunt person to perform the stunt several times until the director is satisfied with the performance.

Stunt performers take great care to ensure their safety. They use air bags, body pads, or cables in stunts involving falls or crashes. If a stunt performer must enter a burning building, he or she wears special fireproof clothing and protective cream on the skin.

Education and Training

No standard training exists for stunt performers. They usually start out by contacting stunt coordinators and asking for work.

If the stunt coordinator thinks the person has the proper credentials, he or she will be hired for basic stunt work like fight scenes.

Stunt performers get a lot of training on the job. Every new type of stunt has its own challenges. By working closely with stunt coordinators, you learn how to eliminate most of the risks involved in stunts. Even so, injuries are very common among stunt performers, and there is even the possibility of death in very dangerous stunts.

Earnings

Stunt performers receive the same day rate as other actors, plus extra pay for more difficult and dangerous stunts. Stunt performers must belong to the actors' union, the Screen Actors Guild (SAG). In 2007, the minimum daily salary of any member of the SAG, including stunt performers, was $759. Stunt coordinators who worked in television productions

EXPLORING

○ Stunt performers must be in top physical shape and train like athletes. To develop your physical strength and coordination, play on community sports teams and participate in school athletics.

○ Acting in school or church plays can teach you about taking direction.

○ Theme parks and circuses use stunt performers. Some of these places allow you to meet the performers after shows.

Famous Daredevils

Stunt performers have been around much longer than the film industry. Throughout the nineteenth century, circus performers leaped from buildings, hung from their necks, walked tightropes, swallowed swords, and stuffed themselves into tiny boxes.

Harry Houdini is one of the most famous showmen in entertainment history. Other daredevils included Samuel Scott, who showed "extraordinary and surpassing powers in the art of leaping and diving." After swinging about a ship's riggings or jumping from a 240-foot cliff, he'd pass around a hat for contributions. His final stunt took place at Waterloo Bridge. While performing predive acrobatics with a rope around his neck, he slipped and strangled to death.

FOR MORE INFO

Visit the SAG's Web site to learn more about a career as a stunt performer.

Screen Actors Guild
5757 Wilshire Boulevard, 7th Floor
Los Angeles, CA 90036-3600
http://www.sag.com

For information on opportunities in the industry, contact the following organizations

Stuntmen's Association of Motion Pictures
10660 Riverside Drive, 2nd Floor, Suite E
Toluca Lake, CA 91602-2352
Tel: 818-766-4334
E-mail: info@stuntmen.com
http://www.stuntmen.com

Stuntwomen's Association of Motion Pictures
Tel: 818-762-0907
E-mail: stuntwomen@stuntwomen.com
http://www.stuntwomen.com

For information about the USA training program, contact

United Stuntmen's Association
10924 Mukilteo Speedway, PMB 272
Mukilteo, WA 98275-5022
Tel: 425-290-9957
http://www.stuntschool.com

earned a daily minimum wage of $759, and a weekly minimum of $2,828.

Outlook

More than 2,500 stunt performers belong to the SAG, but only a small number work on films full time. It is difficult for new stunt performers to break into the business. The future of the profession may be affected by computer technology. Filmmakers today use special effects and computer-generated imagery for action sequences. Computers are also safer. Safety on film sets has always been a serious concern since many stunts are very dangerous. However, using live stunt performers can give a scene more authenticity, so talented stunt performers will always be in demand.

Tour Guides

What Tour Guides Do

Tour guides show visitors around different museums, neighborhoods, cities, and countries. Some tour guides also act as *travel agents* for the tour, booking airline flights, car rentals, and cruises. They research area hotels and other lodgings and plan sightseeing tours. Guides try to meet the needs of the group by learning individual interests.

Many details of each tour are arranged ahead of time, such as hotel reservations, special exhibits, theater tickets, and side trips. There are always problems that arise during trips, though, and guides must be able to handle them quickly and calmly.

Guides make sure that food and lodging meet expected standards and that all baggage and personal belongings are loaded on the plane, bus, or train. It is most important that tour guides keep track of the people on their tours. They must see that everyone returns home safely.

Tour guides know all about the areas they visit. A tour guide on a city tour, for example, knows that city's geography, history, art, architecture, politics, and people. A tour guide for a museum knows every piece in the museum's collection and can explain it clearly to tourists. They are prepared to answer all kinds of questions.

Education and Training

You do not need to earn a college degree to be a tour guide, but it would

It's a Fact

- The U.S. travel and tourism industry generated $1.3 trillion in revenue in 2006.
- There were 7.3 million travel and tourism jobs in 2007. One million of these jobs were related to international tourism to the United States.
- International travelers spent $93 billion in the United States in 2004.

Source: Travel Industry Association of America

EXPLORING

○ Take tours of museums and other special attractions in your area. By listening and observing, you can learn about the work of a tour guide.

○ Join a public speaking or debate club to work on your communication skills.

○ Prepare speeches for class or community groups on local history, architecture, wildlife, or other topics of local interest. Once you have done the research for your speech, you might offer to give a tour to friends or relatives visiting from out of town.

Domestic Travel Stats

○ In 2005, the average traveler was 46 years of age.

○ Domestic travel increased by 12.6 percent from 1995 to 2005.

○ Seventy-five percent of travelers took a trip for pleasure; 25 percent traveled for business.

○ The most popular months to travel were June and July. The least popular months? January and February.

○ The most popular activities for domestic travelers were 1) dining; 2) shopping; and 3) entertainment.

Source: Travel Industry Association of America

be helpful. Courses in history, geography, art, architecture, foreign languages, speech, and communication are good preparation.

Some large cities have professional schools that offer classes in guiding tours. This training may take 9 to 12 months. Some community colleges offer similar training programs that last six to eight weeks. Tour guide training can include classes in geography, psychology, human relations, and communications.

Travel agencies and tour companies often provide their own training, which prepares guides to lead the tours their companies offer.

Earnings

Tour guides usually have busy and slow periods of the year that correspond to vacation and travel seasons. Earnings range from $9.75 to $20 an hour. The average salary for an entry-level tour guide is $20,000. Average mid-level earnings are about $35,000 a year. Experienced guides with managerial responsibilities can earn up to $65,000 a year. The most experienced guides can earn as much as $75,000 annually.

Outlook

Because of the many different travel opportunities for business, recreation, and education, there will be a continuing need for tour guides. Demand will be strongest when the economy is strong (when people earn more money and are able to spend more on travel).

Tours for special interests, such as to conservation areas and wilderness destinations, continue to be popular. Another area of tourism that is growing is inbound tourism. Many foreign travelers visit U.S. tourist spots, such as Hollywood, Disney World, and Yellowstone National Park.

FOR MORE INFO

For information on the travel industry and the related career of travel agent, contact
American Society of Travel Agents
1101 King Street, Suite 200
Alexandria, VA 22314-2963
Tel: 703-739-2782
E-mail: askasta@astahq.com
http://www.astanet.com

For general information on the career of tour guide, contact
National Tour Association
546 East Main Street
Lexington, KY 40508-2342
Tel: 800-682-8886
http://www.ntaonline.com

For information on the travel industry, contact
Travel Industry Association of America
1100 New York Avenue NW, Suite 450
Washington, D.C. 20005-3934
Tel: 202-408-8422
http://www.tia.org/index.html

Glossary

accredited approved as meeting established standards for providing good training and education; this approval is usually given by an independent organization of professionals

apprentice a person who is learning a trade by working under the supervision of a skilled worker; apprentices often receive classroom instruction in addition to their supervised practical experience

associate's degree an academic rank or title granted by a community or junior college or similar institution to graduates of a two-year program of education beyond high school

bachelor's degree an academic rank or title given to a person who has completed a four-year program of study at a college or university. Also called an undergraduate degree or baccalaureate

career an occupation for which a worker receives training and has an opportunity for advancement

certified approved as meeting established requirements for skill, knowledge, and experience in a particular field. People are certified by the organization of professionals in their field

college a higher education institution that is above the high school level

community college a public or private two-year college attended by students who do not usually live at the college. Graduates of a community college receive an associate's degree and may transfer to a four-year college or university to complete a bachelor's degree

diploma   a certificate or document given by a school to show that a person has completed a course or has graduated from the school

distance education a type of educational program that allows students to take classes and complete their education by mail or the Internet

doctorate the highest academic rank or title granted by a graduate school to a person who has completed a two- to three-year program after having received a master's degree

fringe benefit a payment or benefit to an employee in addition to regular wages or salary; examples of fringe benefits include a pension, a paid vacation, and health or life insurance

graduate school a school that people may attend after they have received their bachelor's degree; people who complete an educational program at a graduate school earn a master's degree or a doctorate

intern an advanced student (usually one with at least some college training) in a professional field who is employed in a job that is intended to provide supervised practical experience for the student

internship (1) The position or job of an intern; (2) the period of time when a person is an intern

junior college a two-year college that offers courses like those in the first half of a four-year college program. Graduates of a junior college usually receive an associate's degree and may transfer to a four-year college or university to complete a bachelor's degree

liberal arts the subjects covered by college courses that develop broad general knowledge rather than specific occupational skills. The liberal arts often include philosophy, literature and the arts, history, language, and some courses in the social sciences and natural sciences

licensed   having formal permission from the proper authority to carry out an activity that would be illegal without that permission. For example, a person must be licensed to practice medicine or drive a car

major the academic field in which a college student specializes and receives a degree

master's degree an academic rank or title granted by a graduate school to a person who has completed a one- or two-year program after having received a bachelor's degree

pension an amount of money paid regularly by an employer to a former employee after he or she retires from working

scholarship a gift of money to a student to help the student pay for further education

social studies courses of study (such as civics, geography, and history) that deal with how human societies work

starting salary salary paid to a newly hired employee; the starting salary is usually a smaller amount than is paid to a more experienced worker

technical college a private or public college offering two- or four-year programs in technical subjects; technical colleges offer courses in both general and technical subjects and award associate's degrees and bachelor's degrees

technician a worker with specialized practical training in a mechanical or scientific subject who works under the supervision of scientists, engineers, or other professionals; technicians typically receive two years of college-level education after high school

technologist a worker in a mechanical or scientific field with more training than a technician; technologists typically must have between two and four years of college-level education after high school

undergraduate a student at a college or university who has not yet received a degree

undergraduate degree see **bachelor's degree**

union an organization whose members are workers in a particular industry or company; the union works to gain better wages, benefits, and working conditions for its members; also called a labor union or trade union

vocational school a public or private school that offers training in one or more skills or trades

wage money that is paid in return for work done, especially money paid on the basis of the number of hours or days worked

Index of Job Titles

Browse and Learn More

Books

Ackerman, Thomas H. *FBI Careers: The Ultimate Guide to Landing a Job as One of America's Finest.* 2d ed. Indianapolis, Ind.: JIST Works, 2005.

Bishop, Matt. *Introduction to Computer Security.* Upper Saddle River, N.J.: Addison-Wesley Professional, 2004.

Bullock, Jane A., et al. *Introduction to Homeland Security.* 2nd ed. Burlington, Mass.: Butterworth-Heinemann, 2006.

Cefrey, Holly. *Bounty Hunter.* New York: Children's Press, 2003.

Chaikin, Andrew. *A Man on the Moon: The Voyages of the Apollo Astronauts.* New York: Penguin Books, 2007.

Claybourne, Anna, Gillian Doherty, and Rebecca Treays. *Encyclopedia of Planet Earth.* Tulsa, Okla.: Usborne Publishing, 2000.

Davenport, John C. *Global Extremism and Terrorism.* New York: Chelsea House Publications, 2007.

DK Publishing. *Space Heroes: Amazing Astronauts.* New York: DK Publishing, 2004.

Goldberg, Jan. *Careers in Journalism.* 3d ed. New York: McGraw-Hill, 2005.

Harr, J. Scott, and Karen M. Hess. *Careers in Criminal Justice and Related Fields: From Internship to Promotion.* 5th ed. Belmont, Calif.: Thomson/Wadsworth, 2005.

Hopping, Lorraine. *Bone Detective: The Story of Forensic Anthropologist Diane France.* Washington, D.C.: Joseph Henry Press, 2006.

Millard, Annie. *A Street Through Time.* New York: DK Publishing, 1998.

Needham, Bobbe. *Ecology Crafts For Kids: 50 Great Ways to Make Friends with Planet Earth.* New York: Sterling Publishing, 1998.

Parks, Peggy. *Exploring Careers: Fighter Pilot.* Farmington Hills, Mich.: KidHaven Press, 2005.

———. *Exploring Careers: Firefighter.* Farmington Hills, Mich.: Kid-Haven Press, 2004.

———. *Exploring Careers: Police Officer.* Farmington Hills, Mich.: KidHaven Press, 2003.

Passero, Barbara. *Energy Alternatives.* Farmington Hills, Mich.: Greenhaven Press, 2006.

Peterson's. *Peterson's Summer Opportunities for Kids & Teenagers.* 24th ed. Lawrenceville, N.J.: Peterson's, 2006.

Price, T. Douglas, and Anne Birgitte Gebauer. *Adventures in Fugawiland: A Computerized Simulation in Archaeology.* 3d ed. New York: McGraw-Hill Humanities/Social Sciences/Languages, 2002.

Steele, Philip. *A City Through Time.* New York: DK Publishing, 2004.

Sullivan, George. *In the Line of Fire: Eight Women War Spies.* New York: Scholastic, 1996.

Tyska, Louis A., and Lawrence J. Fennelly. *Investigations: 150 Things You Should Know.* New York: Butterworth-Heineman, 1999.

Wagner, E. J. *The Science of Sherlock Holmes: From Baskerville Hall to the Valley of Fear, the Real Forensics Behind the Great Detective's Greatest Cases.* Hoboken, N.J.: Wiley, 2007.

Wiese, Jim. *Detective Science: 40 Crime-Solving, Case-Breaking, Crook-Catching Activities for Kids.* San Francisco: Jossey-Bass, 1996.

Wolf, Steve. *The Secret Science Behind Movie Stunts & Special Effects.* New York: Skyhorse Publishing, 2007.

Web Sites

American Library Association: Great Web Sites for Kids
http://www.ala.org/greatsites

Bureau of Land Management: Adventures in the Past
http://www.blm.gov/heritage/adventures/vacation.html

Central Intelligence Agency: Kids' Page
https://www.cia.gov/kids-page/index.html

Federal Aviation Administration: Kid's Corner
http://www.faa.gov/education_research/education/student_resources/kids_corner

Federal Bureau of Investigation: Kids' Page
http://www.fbi.gov/fbikids.htm

High School Journalism.org
http://www.highschooljournalism.org

History Detectives
http://pbskids.org/historydetectives/games

National Aeronautics and Space Administration: Astronaut Selection
http://nasajobs.nasa.gov/astronauts

National Fire Protection Association
http://www.nfpa.org

National Geographic Kids
http://kids.nationalgeographic.com

National Park Service: Archeology for Kids
http://www.nps.gov/archeology/public/kids

National Wildlife Federation
http://www.nwf.org

***New York Times* Learning Network**
http://www.nytimes.com/learning

Sierra Club
http://www.sierraclub.org

Smithsonian National Air and Space Museum
http://www.nasm.si.edu

Society for American Archaeology: Archaeology & You
http://www.saa.org/publications/ArchAndYou

SpaceBuffs
http://www.spacebuffs.com

***Time* for Kids**
http://www.timeforkids.com/TFK/kidscoops

U.S. Fire Administration for Kids
http://www.usfa.dhs.gov/kids/flash.shtm